SELF–LEARNING MANAGEMENT SERIES

VIBRANT
PUBLISHERS

SOCIAL MEDIA MARKETING ESSENTIALS

YOU ALWAYS WANTED TO KNOW

Harness the power of social media to market your brand, products, and services.

DR. KAVITA KAMATH

Social Media Marketing Essentials You Always Wanted To Know

First Edition

Paperback ISBN 10: 1–63651–218–6
Paperback ISBN 13: 978–1–63651–218–1

Ebook ISBN 10: 1–63651–219–4
Ebook ISBN 13: 978–1–63651–219–8

Hardback ISBN 10: 1–63651–220–8
Hardback ISBN 13: 978–1–63651–220–4

Library of Congress Control Number: 2023949199

This publication is designed to provide accurate and authoritative information in regard to the subject matter covered. The Author has made every effort in the preparation of this book to ensure the accuracy of the information. However, information in this book is sold without warranty either expressed or implied. The Author or the Publisher will not be liable for any damages caused or alleged to be caused either directly or indirectly by this book.

Vibrant Publishers books are available at special quantity discount for sales promotions, or for use in corporate training programs. For more information please write to bulkorders@vibrantpublishers.com

Please email feedback / corrections (technical, grammatical or spelling) to spellerrors@vibrantpublishers.com

To access the complete catalogue of Vibrant Publishers, visit www.vibrantpublishers.com

SELF-LEARNING MANAGEMENT SERIES

TITLE	PAPERBACK* ISBN

ACCOUNTING, FINANCE & ECONOMICS

COST ACCOUNTING AND MANAGEMENT ESSENTIALS	9781636511030
FINANCIAL ACCOUNTING ESSENTIALS	9781636510972
FINANCIAL MANAGEMENT ESSENTIALS	9781636511009
MACROECONOMICS ESSENTIALS	9781636511818
MICROECONOMICS ESSENTIALS	9781636511153
PERSONAL FINANCE ESSENTIALS	9781636511849

ENTREPRENEURSHIP & STRATEGY

BUSINESS PLAN ESSENTIALS	9781636511214
BUSINESS STRATEGY ESSENTIALS	9781949395778
ENTREPRENEURSHIP ESSENTIALS	9781636511603

GENERAL MANAGEMENT

BUSINESS LAW ESSENTIALS	9781636511702
DECISION MAKING ESSENTIALS	9781636510026
LEADERSHIP ESSENTIALS	9781636510316
PRINCIPLES OF MANAGEMENT ESSENTIALS	9781636511542
TIME MANAGEMENT ESSENTIALS	9781636511665

*Also available in Hardback & Ebook formats

SELF-LEARNING MANAGEMENT SERIES

TITLE	PAPERBACK* ISBN

HUMAN RESOURCE MANAGEMENT

DIVERSITY IN THE WORKPLACE ESSENTIALS	9781636511122
HR ANALYTICS ESSENTIALS	9781636510347
HUMAN RESOURCE MANAGEMENT ESSENTIALS	9781949395839
ORGANIZATIONAL BEHAVIOR ESSENTIALS	9781636510378
ORGANIZATIONAL DEVELOPMENT ESSENTIALS	9781636511481

MARKETING & SALES MANAGEMENT

DIGITAL MARKETING ESSENTIALS	9781949395747
MARKETING MANAGEMENT ESSENTIALS	9781636511788
SALES MANAGEMENT ESSENTIALS	9781636510743
SERVICES MARKETING ESSENTIALS	9781636511733

OPERATIONS & PROJECT MANAGEMENT

AGILE ESSENTIALS	9781636510057
OPERATIONS & SUPPLY CHAIN MANAGEMENT ESSENTIALS	9781949395242
PROJECT MANAGEMENT ESSENTIALS	9781636510712
STAKEHOLDER ENGAGEMENT ESSENTIALS	9781636511511

*Also available in Hardback & Ebook formats

Online Resources

Congratulations! You now have access to practical templates of social media marketing concepts that you will learn in this book. These downloadable templates will help you implement your learnings in the real world and give you an in-depth understanding of the concepts. The templates include:

1. Social Media Calendar

2. Social Media Metrics Calculator for Engagement Rate, Social Share of Voice (SSoV), Response Rate, Conversion Rate, ROI, and Net Promoter Score

To access the templates, follow the steps below:

1. Go to **www.vibrantpublishers.com**

2. Click on the **'Online Resources'** option on the Home Page

3. Login by entering your account details (or create an account if you don't have one)

4. Go to the Self-Learning Management series section on the Online Resources page

5. Click the **'Social Media Marketing Essentials You Always Wanted To Know'** link and access the templates.

Happy self–learning!

This page is intentionally left blank

About the Author

Dr. Kavita Kamath is a faculty member at RMD Sinhgad School of Management Studies, a NAAC 'A++' Accredited institute, affiliated to Savitribai Phule Pune University (SPPU), ranked among the top 10 universities in India. She has a doctorate in social media marketing, an MBA in marketing management, and a bachelor's degree in commerce. She has cleared the National Eligibility Test (UGC-NET) and completed the Strategic Management foundation course from the Indian Institute of Management, Bangalore. She has topped 7 different NPTEL exams conducted by India's premier institutions like IIT and IISC. She has over 18 years of academic and industry experience, having taught various post-graduation courses in management. She has won the Best Employee award at WNS where she worked in market research. She recently won the Best Paper award for her research paper on social media marketing at the 4th International Conference on the Role of Innovation, Entrepreneurship and Management for Sustainable Development, organized by OPJU and Sohar University. She has published her research work in several national and international peer-reviewed journals and has designed the syllabus for 3 courses of Savitribai Phule Pune University's MBA Program. She is also a PhD research guide at SPPU.

This book is dedicated to my raison d'être,
my daughter Divvita.

Her name means 'divine power' and
she has truly enriched my life.

What experts say about this book!

Social Media Marketing Essentials is a must read for anyone wanting to learn about the world of social media either for understanding organic or paid marketing. The 'eyeballs' that are spent on social media only continue to increase making it a key part of any marketing strategy these days. I enjoyed finding the history of these social media companies and the summary of their ad formats, and media measurement metrics in one place! The book provides a good first-principles-based understanding of the key social media platforms - this is really helpful since the social media landscape changes at a really fast pace but once you understand the basics well, it becomes much easier to navigate through the changes whether it's a new content engagement format on an existing network like Instagram or a net new social media network that gains popularity in the next 5 years. Highly recommend this book.

– Mr. Venkatraman Prabhu, Director,
Product Management, Amazon, USA

This book written by Dr. Kavita Kamath Dhumal really captured the purpose of social media marketing in detail and has been written in a simplistic way to teach each and every aspect of marketing-basics to advanced strategies. As a finance person I never knew the intricacies of marketing campaigns and their evaluations but now I understand how every penny spent on various marketing vehicles may translate into revenue.

– Mr. Gannesh Rao, Vice President,
Sony Pictures Networks India

Fantastically written book. It has touched upon all facts and aspects of social media marketing. Aligning to today's market expectations and challenges, it covers important areas of ethics and security to adhere for best practices. One who wishes to synergise social media profession should read this book and try to align with business facts.

– Aniket Asole, Business Growth Leadership in IT

As an academician, I feel a book like this, on one of the most dominant and vital topics of today's business environment, is the need of the hour. The book has a good mix of theory and practical examples which will help readers quickly grasp the concepts. Facebook, YouTube, Instagram, Twitter, Pinterest, LinkedIn, and many more social media platforms have changed the marketing scenario and companies need to jump onto the bandwagon and use Social Media Marketing to grow their business. I would recommend this book to students of marketing, digital marketing, and social media marketing.

– Dr. Kavita Adsule, Business Lecturer,
Global Business Studies

This book is extremely informative and a must-read for anyone looking to learn about social media marketing. The basic concepts, social media strategies and other major concepts have been articulated using simple, easy-to-understand language. It will help readers get a clear understanding of all the essentials of social media marketing and would also benefit small businesses that have either recently adopted social media or plan on doing so. The author has covered all the important concepts, making this an essential read for students and budding digital marketing and social media professionals immensely.

– Dr. Supriya Lakhangaonkar, Director,
Center for Teaching and Learning (CTL), Vishwakarma University

The author has explained all the essentials of social media marketing comprehensively. The simple language along with relevant examples will definitely meet the expectations of students and youngsters looking to learn social media marketing. As a novice in this area, the book truly helped me understand the various facets of social media marketing. I especially enjoyed reading about social media strategies which, in my opinion, can be of benefit to small businesses as well. Also, the chapter on ethics was truly insightful, as our young generation needs to understand the importance of ethics in all aspects of life.The book can be used by beginners to gain a fundamental understanding of the subject before digging deeper into its various aspects. This book also aligns well with the contemporary social media marketing syllabus of our University and will help subject teachers teach this subject effectively to our young students.

– Ravindra Deshmukh, Professor & Head,
Department of Commerce & Research Center, Ahmednagar College

The book is divided into 8 chapters covering social media marketing strategies, measurement metrics and ethical practices. The author has rightly identified the target audience and designed the content and flow of the text in a very smooth and interesting way. By introducing the reader to major social media platforms in the initial chapter, the author navigates through the journey of social media marketing practised by these platforms further into the book. Media marketing matrices – terms like engagement rate, social share of voice, ROI, audience growth rate, NPS, etc have been elaborated in lucid language. Fun facts, quizzes, flow charts and real life examples ensure an immersive reading. I definitely recommend this book.

– Dr Milind A Marathe, Professor,
Sinhgad Institute of Management and Computer Applications

Simplification of any topic is the key and this book is easy to read, understand and comprehend the subject. It is informative yet compact, engaging and interactive by way of a quiz at the end of each chapter. It's a practical guide that deals with the A to Z of social media marketing and its landscape that one can relate to in that particular geography. Dr. Kavita Kamath has chapters devoted to the description of social media platforms and has showcased relevant examples; this depicts the efforts taken to develop these chapters and then organize it in such a manner that every chapter ends with an excitement that hooks you to the next chapter.

– Uday Zokarkar, Founder & CEO,
Mantra Media Private Limited

Social Media Marketing Essentials You Always Wanted to Know, by Kavita Kamath delivers on the author's titular promise. I found this book organized and easy to follow and highly recommend it to those looking to up their social media game!

– Tara Leigh, Book Trade Professional,
Hachette & St. Martin's Press, United States

Table of Contents

This page is intentionally left blank

Acknowledgement

This book wouldn't have been possible without the guidance, support and help received from many people.

I would like to thank the entire team at Vibrant Publishers for being extremely supportive and understanding and helping this book become a better version of itself.

I express my heartfelt gratitude to my uncle and aunt, Mr. Radhakrishna Prabhu and Mrs. Mangala Prabhu for giving me the greatest gift one can receive, education. They have helped me become independent and able to stand on my own feet. My biggest strength has been my mother, who has fought against all odds to give me the best opportunities. Her sacrifices, determination, and constant, unwavering belief in me have been my guiding light in this journey. I'd also like to thank my husband, Dilip for motivating me to achieve newer heights and letting me be myself. And I'd like to acknowledge the sunshine of my life, my daughter Divvita, who just by being in my life, has made me happy and content, thereby being able to concentrate better on my professional assignments.

I'd also like to thank Mr. Aniruddha Patil, founder of PEO, for sharing his story with me, which helped me pen the wonderful case study of his journey for this book.

I'd also like to express my immense gratitude towards all the reviewers who spared their valuable time and efforts for reading the book and providing their valuable feedback. Finally, a big thank you to all my friends, colleagues, and family members who have helped me in many ways while writing this book.

This page is intentionally left blank

Disclaimer

All costs mentioned in the book are as of 2023; social media is a dynamic field, hence costs may keep changing. They have been mentioned here specifically for representational purposes so that readers can get a comparative view of various media.

This page is intentionally left blank

Preface

When doing my Ph.D. in social media marketing, I tried to get my hands on as many books on social media as I could that would help me better understand this topic. While I found that there were many books on social media marketing targeted toward businesses looking to expand their social media presence, I felt there was a lack of one that explains the basics of social media marketing, especially to beginners looking to understand the concepts, build a career in this field, or small businesses looking to grow through social media. Having spent over 15 years in academia, teaching marketing has helped me understand the needs of students and young professionals. My job involves several interactions with industry professionals, and when I met experts from the marketing and media sector, the conversation would invariably lead to discussions about social media marketing, as the current marketing landscape is incomplete without it. That is when the idea of writing a book encompassing all the basics of social media marketing started taking shape in my mind. Thus began my association with Vibrant Publishers for my first book titled "Social Media Marketing Essentials You Always Wanted to Know".

This book aims to be a guide to anyone looking to understand what social media marketing is, what it entails, its characteristics, scope, importance, and types of social media platforms. With the help of simple examples, statistics, and detailed explanations of various concepts, this book will serve to help all students, budding social media professionals, and businesses alike. The journey of penning this book has been truly enriching and uplifting as I got the opportunity to interact and learn from various industry experts, small business owners, my fellow academicians and students. Their inputs have helped shape this book. I hope you enjoy reading this book as much as I enjoyed writing it. Happy learning!

This page is intentionally left blank

Introduction to the book

The world around us has rapidly changed from physical to digital. The colossal transformations that technology has undergone and their impact on marketing practices are incredible. The traditional market consisted of a physical place where marketing activities took place, most of which were one-sided, time-consuming, and at times, lacked time and place utility. The advent of social media has changed all that, and how! The economy has now become digital and social media marketing has revolutionized marketing practices. With handheld devices, customers today have access to everything at their fingertips. Social media has permeated into our lives in such a manner that it is now an integral part of our digital lives.

Businesses today are constantly looking to increase and improve their brand presence online and leverage social media to market their products more effectively. Social media allows businesses to create brand awareness and differentiation, build their brand image, engage with their customers, and deliver superior value to them, thus resulting in enhanced customer satisfaction. Since more and more businesses are turning to social media and integrating it into their media mixes, the need for social media marketing professionals is surging.

This book intends to study the phenomenon of social media and takes one through all its essentials. The book will help you acquire clarity about the following:

- What is social media? What is social media marketing?
- What are its benefits and limitations?
- What is the scope of social media and how can it be used?

- What are the essential concepts and terminologies in social media?

- Which are the various social media platforms and how are they different from each other? What are they used for in terms of marketing?

- How to leverage social media for one's business?

- What are the ethical issues and best practices in social media marketing?

- What parameters should be used to evaluate the effectiveness and impact of social media marketing programs?

How to use this book?

This book can be used as a reference guide to understand the role and relevance of social media marketing to businesses in the current marketing environment.

1. If you are an amateur in social media marketing and have just a basic idea about social media, Chapter 1 will help you know a little more like its origins, various platforms, and their features.

2. To learn and understand how social media differs from traditional media and its advantages and disadvantages chapter 2 is your go-to. It will also help you understand the concepts of paid and organic marketing along with influencer marketing and how to conduct competitor analysis using social media.

3. If you are a small business and want to plan your social media marketing activities and set a social media strategy, chapter 3 will prove beneficial.

4. Chapter 4 acts as a guide to all those who want to learn about content designing for various social media platforms, i.e. the kinds of content and the various tools available for designing quality.

5. If you want to learn about marketing on Facebook, Instagram, Threads, X (formerly Twitter), YouTube, LinkedIn, and Pinterest read Chapters 1, 5, and 6.

6. If you are using social media marketing and want to evaluate its effectiveness for your business, read Chapter 7, which talks about the various metrics which help evaluate the effectiveness of social media marketing campaigns.

7. Finally, read Chapter 8 to learn about the best ethical practices for social media marketing.

This page is intentionally left blank

Who can benefit from this book?

1. Students interested in building a career in social media marketing or digital marketing.

2. Businesses looking to adopt social media into their marketing strategy and learn how to leverage it for marketing one's business.

3. Social media managers and professionals with limited exposure to the latest trends, processes, and basics of social media marketing or those who want a deeper understanding of the essentials of social media marketing.

4. Anyone with a desire to know more about social media marketing, its importance, the processes involved, the ethics that surround the domain, and the strategies needed for effective execution.

This page is intentionally left blank

Chapter **1**

Introduction to Social Media

Social media is a phenomenon that has changed the world in unprecedented ways. With its growing popularity among users, social media has become an indispensable tool for marketers around the world. Chapter 1 explains the concept of social media, and delves into its history and evolution. The chapter further describes the various social media platforms along with their features. The purpose is to ensure that the readers understand the definition and evolutionary progress of social media and also learn about the major social media platforms.

The key learning objectives should include the reader's understanding of the following:

- The concept of social media, its characteristics, and scope

- The history and evolution of social media

- Features of various social media platforms: Facebook, Instagram, Threads, YouTube, Twitter, Pinterest, LinkedIn

1.1 Introduction to Social Media

Today, in the era of globalization, many dynamic changes are taking place in the business environment. One such change is the advent of social media and its growing popularity. Social media has grown due to the emergence of social networking sites like Facebook, Twitter, YouTube, LinkedIn, Instagram, Google+, etc.

Mangold & Faulds (2009)[1] have defined social media in the following words: "Social media encompasses a wide range of online, word-of-mouth forums including blogs, company-sponsored discussion boards and chat rooms, consumer-to-consumer e-mail, consumer product or service ratings websites and forums, Internet discussion boards and forums, blogs (sites containing digital audio, images, movies, or photographs), and social networking websites, to name a few."

Andreas Kaplan and Michael Haenlein[2] define social media as "a group of Internet-based applications that build on the ideological and technological foundations of Web 2.0, and that allow the creation and exchange of user-generated content."

In the elaboration of this definition, the authors explain that Web 2.0 is defined by the way it is used, viz. users creating and exchanging content. What differentiates Web 2.0 from Web 1.0 (which is the earliest form of the internet) is that the users can create content such as images, videos, text, graphics, etc., and

---

1. W. Glynn Mangold and David J. Faulds, "Social Media: The New Hybrid Element of the Promotion Mix," *Business Horizons* 52, no. 4 (July 1, 2009): 357–65, https://doi.org/10.1016/j.bushor.2009.03.002.

2. Andreas Kaplan and Michael Haenlein, "Users of the World, Unite! The Challenges and Opportunities of Social Media," *Business Horizons* 53, no. 1 (January 1, 2010): 59–68, https://doi.org/10.1016/j.bushor.2009.09.003.

share it with other users. This includes using the World Wide Web as a collaborative and participatory platform for creating, sharing, and using content as opposed to individuals creating and publishing content. The term Web 2.0 was first used in 2004 to describe a new way in which software developers and end users started using the World Wide Web. It has now become a platform where content and applications are not created and shared by individuals but are continuously updated and modified by users in a participatory and collaborative manner. Kaplan and Haenlein[3] say that Web 2.0 is the platform for the evolution of social media.

The above definitions imply that social media is a group of websites or web pages and applications that allow users to create content and share it. They can share their thoughts, ideas, pictures, and expressions and publish them. This content is accessible to all or selective users, thus making any social media platform an open forum. Various users can interact with one another using social media as it provides an interactive platform.

Alan Charlesworth[4] defines social media as "any web presence where users can add their own content but do not have control over the site in the same way as they would have over their own website." You can post content, edit it, post reviews, give feedback, register complaints, ask queries, and give remarks. However, control of the site does not lie in your hands. Social media is thus an *engagement* tool where users engage by sharing content.

Social media is gaining momentum in countries all over the world, mainly due to the emergence of social media networks. The

---

3. Loc. cit.

4. Alan Charlesworth, An Introduction to Social Media Marketing, Routledge eBooks, 2014, https://doi.org/10.4324/9780203727836.

nature of social media is quite different from that of traditional media. Social media is online whereas traditional media is offline, hence it is also known as offline media. Most of the traditional media is based on one-way communication. Social media, on the other hand, enables quick feedback and multi-way communication.

Fun Facts:

- The average American spends 2.7 hours per day on social media.[5]

- 2,460,000 pieces of content are shared on Facebook every second.[6]

- Over 16 billion photos have been uploaded on Instagram since its inception.[7]

- Almost 41% of millionaires use LinkedIn.[8]

- 77% of B2B companies have obtained new customers through Facebook.[9]

5. Trevin Shirey and Trevin Shirey, "8 Surprising Social Media Marketing Facts," WebFX, n.d., https://www.webfx.com/blog/social-media/8-surprising-social-media-facts/.

6. Penguin Team, "68 Social Media Facts & Stats That Will Blow Your Mind," PenguinStrategies, August 3, 2023, https://www.penguinstrategies.com/blog/68-social-media-facts-stats-media-that-will-blow-your-mind.

7. Hiram Ting et al., "Beliefs about the Use of Instagram: An Exploratory Study," ResearchGate, January 1, 2015, https://www.researchgate.net/publication/272026006_Beliefs_about_the_Use_of_Instagram_An_Exploratory_Study.

8. Natalia Wiechowski, "LinkedIn Demystified & Explained: Mind-Blowing Stats, FAQs and Stories," June 21, 2020, https://www.linkedin.com/pulse/linkedin-demystified-explained-mind-blowing-stats-faqs-wiechowski.

9. Christina Newberry, "42 Facebook Statistics Marketers Need to Know in 2023," Social Media Marketing & Management Dashboard, July 5, 2023, https://blog.hootsuite.com/facebook-statistics/.

- India has the largest number of Facebook users country-wise with over 320 million users.[10]

1.1.1 Characteristics of Social Media

A Web 2.0 application

Web 1.0 allowed users to send one-way communication to others. Web 2.0 took things further by allowing multi-way communication. It enables user created content to be shared with multiple people. Rather than being a new version of the web, Web 2.0 is the use of more user generated content along with social interaction on the web. Social media is an innovation born out of Web 2.0. Social media allows users to generate content using various social media platforms. This content can be shared and commented on by other users.

Example: Facebook allows users to create and share posts, videos, images which other users can comment on and share further.

User generated Content

User-generated content is also called user-created content. It includes any type of content, like text, images, audios and videos that has been posted by users on social media platforms. Social media enables users to generate content in the form of posts, blogs, vlogs, videos, reels, podcasts, comments, etc. This content

---

10. Svetlana Valitova, "Countries with the Most Facebook Users 2023," Ecwid | E-Commerce Shopping Cart, April 28, 2023, https://www.ecwid.com/insights/facebook-countries-with-the-users#:~:text=Most%20active%20Facebook%20users%20in%20India%3A%20329.65%20millions.

can further be shared by the users with other users.

Interactive

Social media is highly interactive, enabling two-way and multi-way communication. The creator of the content can communicate with other users, who can communicate with the creator too. The users can interact with one another as well. Let's take an example to understand this. Suppose Pepsi shares a post on Facebook which includes a video of their product along with its latest advertising campaign. Users can comment whether they like the ad, their thoughts and experiences with Pepsi. Pepsi in turn can reply to all these users. The users can like and comment on other users' comments too, making it a multi-way communication.

High Reach

With an increasing number of people using social media, social media today has a huge reach. According to globalstatistics.com[11], in 2024, there are 246.0 million active social media users in the United States of America, which is a whopping 72.5% of the total population of US. Globally too, social media users are increasing at a speedy rate. This has made social media an extremely important tool for marketers, as by using its high reach, they can target their prospective customers and large section of the population.

---

11. The Global Statistics. "US Social Media Statistics 2024 | Most Popular Platform in US," January 7, 2024. https://www.theglobalstatistics.com/united-states-social-media-statistics/

Easy to Access

Social media is relatively easier to access, as these days, anyone who owns a phone and an internet connection can access social media. They just need to create a profile by providing their basic information and they can immediately start creating and sharing content as well as accessing content of their interests. Most of the content posted is uncensored, and easily accessible. Users can visit the brand pages and read the content as well as post their comments or comment on other user's comments and have discussions.

1.1.2 Scope of Social Media

We have witnessed an enormous increase in the number of social media users in the past years. Various studies show that there are over 270 million social media users in the US as of 2022. That means almost 81% of America's population is using social media. China has the highest number of social media users in the world, followed by India. The US ranks 3rd and its number of social media users is growing rapidly. This shows that social media has a vast scope in the US.

Globally too, the world has seen an equally rapid increase in the number of social media users. There were 4.59 billion social media users in the world in 2022. This number is expected to increase to 5.85 billion in the next five years.

This sort of growth shows that social media has tremendous potential for marketers and businesses all over the world who wish to reach their target market more effectively.

| Figure 1.1 | Number of social media users worldwide |

Number of social media users worldwide from 2017 to 2027 (*in billions*)

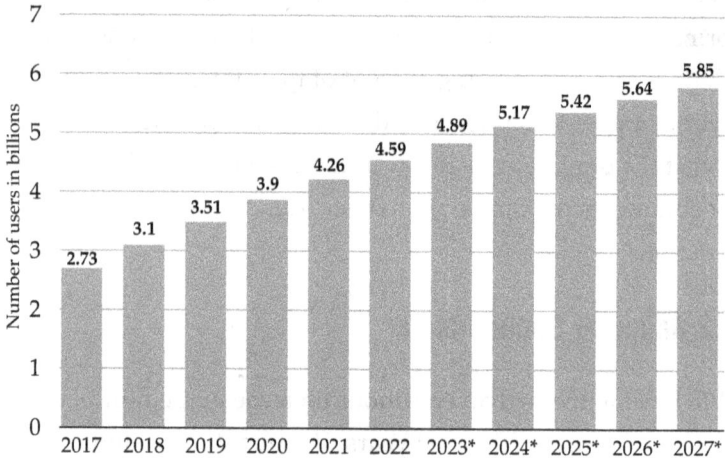

Number of users in billions

Year	Value
2017	2.73
2018	3.1
2019	3.51
2020	3.9
2021	4.26
2022	4.59
2023*	4.89
2024*	5.17
2025*	5.42
2026*	5.64
2027*	5.85

Source: https://www.statista.com/statistics/278414/number-of-worldwide-social-network-users/

1.2 History of Social Media

The history of social media can be traced back to the history of communication and the advent of the internet. When the internet was invented, it drastically changed the world of communication. Human beings have always been social animals and have always had the impulse to communicate. We generally like to share our feelings and emotions with our family, friends, colleagues, neighbors, etc. When we achieve something great or win accolades, we like to tell others about it and be congratulated or appreciated. We like to share our milestones with our loved ones. The evolution of social media lies therein. It is about enhancing these personal communications, albeit on a larger scale and with the help of digital technology.

Six Degrees, created in 1997 by Andrew Weinreich, was the first social media platform. It was used for social networking with friends, family, and acquaintances but shut down its operations by 2001.

In 1999, many blogging sites were developed and gained popularity. From 2003 onward, many new SNSs (Social Networking Service) were launched, prompting social software analyst Clay Shirky (2003) to coin the term YASNS: "Yet Another Social Networking Service."[12]

Google+ was a social networking site operated by Google. On October 8, 2018, Google announced that it was shutting down Google+ for consumers because of low user engagement and a software error, first reported by The Wall Street Journal[13], that potentially exposed the data of hundreds of thousands of users. Google, prior to Google+, had launched Orkut in 2004, which was another social media platform that ran for around 10 years before getting shut down in 2014.

Friendster, founded in 2002, is considered to be the "first modern social media" platform. It was the brainchild of Jonathan Abrams and was created as a place where users could do gaming and networking. Friendster helped users discover friends and expand their social network. Friendster went on a break in 2015 to focus on improving its services.

---

12. Danah Boyd and Nicole B. Ellison, "Social Network Sites: Definition, History, and Scholarship," Journal of Computer-Mediated Communication 13, no. 1 (October 1, 2007): 210–30, https://doi.org/10.1111/j.1083-6101.2007.00393.x.
13. MacMillan, Douglas; McMillan, Robert. "Google Exposed User Data, Feared Repercussions of Disclosing to Public". The Wall Street Journal. October 16, 2018.

Hi5, launched in 2003, is an American social networking site headquartered in San Francisco, California. It was founded by Ramu Yalamanchi and Akash Garg. Currently, it has more than one million active users. Its popularity is high in Asia, Central Africa, and Latin America.

In 2003, LinkedIn was founded in Mountain View, California by Reid Hoffman, Allen Blue, Konstantin Guericke, Eric Ly, and Jean-Luc Vaillant. It is mainly used for career development and professional networking. Since December 2016, it has been a wholly-owned subsidiary of Microsoft. As of 2022, LinkedIn has over 830 million registered users worldwide.

In 2004, Facebook was launched at Harvard. Initially, membership was restricted to only Harvard students. But with time, it swiftly started spreading to other schools. By 2008, it had gained massive popularity as a social media platform. It is currently the most popular and most used social media platform across the world. As of 2023, Facebook remains the most popular social media platform among customers as well as businesses.

YouTube, a video-sharing social media platform was founded in February 2005 by former PayPal employees Chad Hurley, Steve Chan, and Jawed Karim. It is headquartered in San Bruno, California. Google purchased YouTube in 2006 and it is currently the most popular video-sharing social media platform.

Twitter was launched in 2006. While it was initially designed as a mobile SMS platform, since then it has upgraded and is a social media platform where users can send messages. It allowed users to post and share short messages of 140 characters, popularly known as "tweets". From November 2017, the number of characters that could be used was doubled. According to the company's last investor earnings report, Twitter had a total of

238 million monetizable daily active users around the world. On October 27, 2022, Twitter was acquired by Elon Musk for $44 billion. On July 23, 2023, Twitter was rebranded to "X".

In 2010, Instagram was launched into the public domain by Kevin Systrom and was soon acquired by Facebook in 2011. Initially launched as a photo-sharing website, it now allows users to upload and share photos and video stories. It is today the world's most visited photo and video-sharing website.

On July 5th, 2023, Meta launched Threads, a new social media app, built by the Instagram team. Threads can be used for sharing text updates and joining public conversations. Users can log in using their Instagram account and posts can be up to 500 characters long and include links, photos, and videos up to five minutes in length. Meta is planning to make Threads compatible with ActivityPub. ActivityPub is an open social networking protocol that has been established by the World Wide Web Consortium (W3C), the body responsible for the open standards that power the modern web.[14]

In 2010, Ben Silberman, Paul Sciarra, and Evan Sharp founded Pinterest. It was launched as a virtual pinboard and has since garnered more than 400 million registered users worldwide. It became a public trading company in 2019. It is used for image sharing and enables users to save and discover information on the internet using images, animated GIFs, and videos in the form of pinboards.

Today, there are numerous social media platforms and technological advancements have made them accessible to people

---

14. Facebook Company and Meta, "Introducing Threads: A New Way to Share with Text," Meta, October 26, 2023, https://about.fb.com/news/2023/07/introducing-threads-new-app-text-sharing/.

across the globe. With more than half of the world using social media, it has come a long way and continues to grow rapidly. It has therefore emerged as an important tool for advertisers across the world who are increasingly using social media along with traditional media like television, newspapers, and radio.

Figure 1.2 Evolution of social media

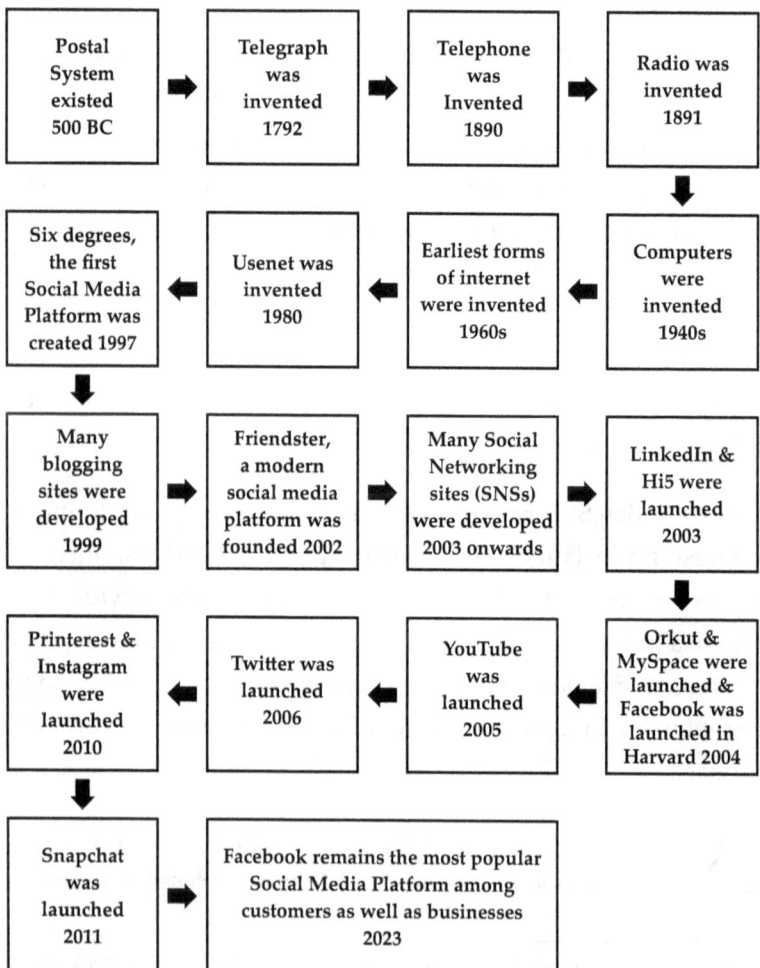

Postal System existed 500 BC ➡	Telegraph was invented 1792 ➡	Telephone was Invented 1890 ➡	Radio was invented 1891 ⬇
Six degrees, the first Social Media Platform was created 1997 ⬅	Usenet was invented 1980 ⬅	Earliest forms of internet were invented 1960s ⬅	Computers were invented 1940s
⬇ Many blogging sites were developed 1999 ➡	Friendster, a modern social media platform was founded 2002 ➡	Many Social Networking sites (SNSs) were developed 2003 onwards ➡	LinkedIn & Hi5 were launched 2003 ⬇
Printerest & Instagram were launched 2010 ⬅	Twitter was launched 2006 ⬅	YouTube was launched 2005 ⬅	Orkut & MySpace were launched & Facebook was launched in Harvard 2004
⬇ Snapchat was launched 2011 ➡	Facebook remains the most popular Social Media Platform among customers as well as businesses 2023		

1.3 Major Social Media Platforms

1.3.1 Facebook

As discussed above, Facebook remains the most popular social media platform among users and businesses alike.

Facebook is an online social media site used mainly for social networking. It is owned by an American company called Meta Platforms. Facebook was founded in 2004 by Mark Zuckerberg (current CEO) along with his Harvard collegemates Eduardo Saverin, Andrew McCollum, Dustin Moskovitz, and Chris Hughes. They called it Facebook based on the facebook directories that American university students often get. Initially, membership of Facebook was limited exclusively to Harvard students, but based on its growing popularity, they later expanded it to other North American universities. Starting in 2006, anyone over 13 years old could open a Facebook account. In the second quarter of 2022, Facebook claimed to have over 2.93 billion monthly active users. India has the largest number of Facebook users, followed by the United States, Indonesia, Brazil, and Mexico respectively.

Some features of Facebook are:

1. You can post text, photos, videos, live videos, GIFs, emojis, and more which are shared with other users who have agreed to be your "friend".

2. You can customize the privacy settings of your profile and your posts to control who can see them.

3. Facebook offers a "Like Button" where you can like posts and other multimedia. The more likes a page or post receives, the more popular it supposedly is.

4. You can also communicate directly with other people using Facebook Messenger.

5. You receive notifications related to the activities of your Facebook friends.

6. You can also join mutual groups of interest that post the content you like. There are Facebook pages Harry Potter fans, dog lovers, foodies, restaurateurs and even local communities.

1.3.2 Instagram

Instagram is a photo and video-sharing social media platform founded by Kevin Systrom and Mike Krieger in 2010. Just short of its two-year mark, on April 9, 2012, it was acquired by Facebook Inc. (currently Meta Platforms). Instagram's popularity soared in June 2013, when video sharing was introduced. Currently, Adam Mosseri is the head of Instagram.

With three in five adults from the US using Instagram, it is one of the most popular social networking platforms in the US. Globally too, Instagram's popularity is reaching new heights. They recorded more than two billion monthly users worldwide in December 2021, according to a CNBC report.[15]

---

15. Salvador Rodriguez, "Instagram Surpasses 2 Billion Monthly Users While Powering through a Year of Turmoil," CNBC, December 14, 2021, https://www.cnbc.com/2021/12/14/instagram-surpasses-2-billion-monthly-users.html.

On Instagram:

1. You can edit and upload photos and reels (short videos) on your account

2. You can use filters to make various changes to your photos, like adding a cool or warm tone to the image, making it brighter with more light, changing the image saturation, and lots more.

3. You have the option to follow other users' feeds and receive post-notification alerts.

4. You can connect your Instagram accounts to other social media platforms, thus enabling you to share uploaded photos and videos to multiple sites simultaneously.

5. Users can easily interact with each other through the comments section. Instagram also offers a feature called Live, which allows you to start a live broadcast where you can invite up to three people to go live with.

Instagram, on its website, says that it helps brands generate leads, increase their brand awareness, and target the right audience. There are more than two million businesses that connect with their customers using Instagram. Instagram offers various options to businesses for marketing their products and services: paid ads, videos, images, reels, shopping, etc. 22% of millennials have ranked Instagram as their favorite social media platform. Hence, this has resulted in many social media marketing professionals at fashionable boutiques and high-end cosmetic companies flocking to the platform.[16]

---

16. Claire Brenner, "What Is Instagram Marketing? (+7 Instagram Posts That Perform)," July 26, 2018, https://learn.g2.com/instagram-marketing.

1.3.3 Threads

Threads is a social media platform introduced by Meta Platforms. It is closely linked to Instagram and requires users to have an Instagram handle, which they need to use to log in to Threads. It functions similarly to Twitter and has the same community guidelines as Instagram. Threads reached 100 million users within five days of its launch making it the fastest social media platform to do so. Posts are known as threads. You can reply to, repost, and like threads. Threads can be up to 500 text characters or videos upto five minutes. Threads is compared to Twitter, pitting them as competitors.

As of August 2023, Threads and Instagram accounts share the same username, profile picture, and display name by default. However, the display name and profile picture can be customized. Moreover, if you wish to delete your Threads account, you need to delete the associated Instagram account too.

As Threads is fairly new, it will be undergoing various changes and updates in the coming days.

1.3.4 YouTube

YouTube was founded in February 2005 and emerged as one of the first major video-sharing sites. Google purchased the site in November 2006 for $1.65 billion and now functions as one of Google's subsidiaries. Using YouTube, users can upload, download, and watch videos, rate and share them, report offensive content, post comments on videos, and subscribe to other "channels". There is a wide variety of user-generated videos, documentaries, movie trailers, short films, movies, TV show clips, live streams, video blogs, music videos, etc. available on YouTube.

After being acquired by Google, YouTube's revenue generation model was expanded to include exclusive content that is ad-free under a paid subscription to YouTube Premium and access to paid content like movies. This was contrary to its earlier business plan, in which revenue was generated through advertisements only. Susan Wojcicki was the CEO of YouTube. Neal Mohan succeeded Susan Wojcicki as YouTube's CEO on February 16, 2023.

Some key features of YouTube are:

1. As a YouTube user, you are usually allowed to upload videos that are up to 15 minutes long. Once your account is verified, you can upload videos of up to 12 hours in duration, along with producing live streams.

2. In 2018, a new feature known as Premiere was added on YouTube. It allows accounts to notify other accounts when an upcoming video is launched. The account owner has to manually opt to receive the notification. This is similar to a live stream but except that it is a pre-recorded video. At the specified or scheduled time, the video is aired in the form of a live broadcast following a two-minute countdown. A premiere can also be scheduled instantly.

3. To compete against TikTok, a Chinese video hosting app featuring short videos ranging from 15 seconds to 10 minutes, YouTube Shorts was launched in 2020. The time limit for videos on YouTube shorts is 60 seconds.

YouTube has more than 2.5 billion monthly active users worldwide including more than 30 million paid subscribers using YouTube Premium and Music services. This means that YouTube is accessed by approximately one-fourth of the world's population. In the US, the number of YouTube users is expected to reach 210 million. Of all the social media platforms, only Facebook has more users than YouTube. T-Series, an Indian music video channel, is the most subscribed channel on YouTube with more than 249 million subscribers.

1.3.5 X (Formerly "Twitter")

Twitter is a microblogging and social networking service offered by Twitter Inc., a company incorporated in California. Twitter was founded by Jack Dorsey, Noah Glass, Biz Stone, and Evan Williams and launched in July 2006. Parag Agrawal was its CEO till October 2022. On April 14, 2022, Elon Musk initiated a takeover of Twitter which ended on October 27, 2022. In a $44 billion deal, Elon Musk acquired Twitter. Linda Yaccarino succeeded Musk as the CEO of Twitter on June 5, 2023. Musk's acquisition of Twitter was followed by several drastic changes such as firing almost half of its workforce, changing the character limit of tweets, charging a fee for verified accounts, and rebranding Twitter altogether. From July 23, 2023, Twitter has been rebranded to "X".

Following are some of the key features of X (formerly Twitter):

1. X users can "tweet" or post their thoughts which are short messages to communicate with their followers.

2. Before rebranding, a tweet could be 140 characters long. The limit was increased to 280 characters later. The short character length of tweets makes them appealing to the current generation who consume content like fast food. 4. Twitter Blue (a premium version of Twitter) users can post tweets up to 4000 characters long.

3. Twitter is simple to use. You can either be a broadcaster or a receiver. You can join with a free account and create a Twitter (now X) name. You can then post tweets either daily, hourly, or as frequently as you want.

4. X also gives you an option to block people for your privacy.

5. Businesses can use X to share the company's thoughts, special achievements, advertising and marketing messages, product information, clarifications, and a lot more with their followers and customers.

6. If followers find tweets of brands/companies/people they follow not as interesting as they expected, they can unfollow them.

Within just three years of its inception, X, (previously Twitter) achieved one billion total tweets on its platform. X is among the top social media sites in the US and has over 400 million users. With its huge user base, Twitter has gained popularity among marketers who are looking to expand their brand presence online. A study showed that around 33% of users use Twitter to follow brands or companies.[17]

Although Twitter (now X) has fewer users than Facebook, Instagram, YouTube, and Pinterest, it has over 200 million active daily users who come back to check daily updates. This makes it an important tool for marketers to reach a large audience.

---

17. Social Shepherd Ltd, "23 Essential Twitter Statistics You Need to Know in 2023," The Social Shepherd, May 16, 2023, https://thesocialshepherd.com/blog/twitter-statistics.

1.3.6 Pinterest

Pinterest is a visual social media platform and image-sharing service. Within a year of its launch, Pinterest was listed among the 50 best websites of that year by Time magazine. Pinterest describes itself as a visual discovery engine that helps users find ideas like recipes, designs, styles, etc. Bill Ready is currently its CEO.

Let's take a look at a few key features of Pinterest:

1. Pinterest mainly contains "pins" and "boards". A "pin" is a bookmark that people use to save the content they like on Pinterest. It can be an image that has been uploaded or linked from a website. A "board" is nothing but an individual's collection of pins.

2. You can also "re-pin" another user's pin to your own board.

3. You can also upload content found outside Pinterest to a board using the "Save" button, which can be used as part of a downloadable extension on a web browser. Boards can be dedicated to themes like dress styles, home furnishing ideas, travel images, party decorations, and anything else that you can think of.

4. Users can follow and unfollow boards as well as each other

An interesting fact is that most of Pinterest's users are women. It is the fourth most popular social media platform in the United States. Moreover, more than 87% of users have bought a product because of Pinterest,[18] which opens up avenues for marketing. Marketers can use Pinterest to post appealing pictures of their

---

18. Saige Driver, "Pinterest for Business: Everything You Need to Know," Business News Daily, October 24, 2023, https://www.businessnewsdaily.com/7552-pinterest-business-guide.html.

products/brands to attract their target market as well as reach out to a large audience.

In Quarter 4 of 2021, Pinterest reported a revenue growth of 20% mainly due to increased demand from retail advertisers.[19] Marketers can upload or "pin" their product/brand content to Pinterest, then re-pin by sharing the content and keep customers engaged by having them like their pins.

1.3.7 LinkedIn

LinkedIn is unique from all the other social media platforms discussed above in the sense that it is employment-oriented and is focused mainly on career development and professional development. LinkedIn's mission is to "Connect the world's professionals to make them more productive and successful".[20] LinkedIn has been created for the business community. Using LinkedIn, registered members can create networks with people they know and trust professionally.

Here are a few features of LinkedIn:

1. Unlike other free social networking sites like Facebook or Twitter, LinkedIn is a professional social networking site, where professionals can look for jobs, connect with domain experts, research companies, and gather information and news about the industry and businesses.

---

19. Staff Correspondent, "Pinterest (PINS): A Few Points to Keep in Mind If You Have an Eye on This Stock," AlphaStreet, March 15, 2022, https://news.alphastreet.com/pinterest-pins-a-few-points-to-keep-in-mind-if-you-have-an-eye-on-this-stock/.
20. "About LinkedIn," About LinkedIn, n.d., https://about.linkedin.com/.

2. You get access to a basic membership which is free, using which you can only establish connections with people you know professionally, and people you have worked with or have gone to school with. These people become a part of your network and are known as "connections".

3. LinkedIn connections are classified into three parts: 1st, 2nd, and 3rd degree connections. 1st degree connections include people who are connected to you directly through invitations. 2nd degree connections are those whom you know through a mutual connection. People with whom one shares extended network connections are known as 3rd-degree connections.

4. LinkedIn provides premium membership (paid service) for better network connections and additional features.

5. Businesses use LinkedIn to access decision makers and build connections with them, engage customers with LinkedIn Messaging, and share information about the company, its achievements, products, brands, and marketing programs. They can also advertise on LinkedIn.

LinkedIn currently has over 930 million members worldwide[21] including over 58 million registered companies. Of these, 310 million are monthly active users.[22] Out of its frequent users, 40% access it daily, taking its interactions to over one billion each month. Over 185 million users of LinkedIn are from the United States. With a wide presence in over 200 countries and regions, LinkedIn is an important tool for marketers.[23]

---

21. Ibid.

22. "LinkedIn Statistics - 2023 Update | 99Firms," n.d., https://99firms.com/blog/linkedin-statistics/#gref.

23. Hannah Macready, "47 LinkedIn Statistics You Need To Know In 2023," Social Media Marketing & Management Dashboard, July 5, 2023, https://blog.hootsuite.com/linkedin-statistics-business/.

Fun Facts:

- Mark Zuckerberg initially wanted to name Facebook "Facemash".[24]

- Almost 1100 photos are uploaded on Instagram every second.[25]

- More than one billion hours of videos are watched on YouTube every day.[26]

- With more than 140 million followers, Elon Musk is the most followed person on X.[27]

- LinkedIn has almost 60 million organizations on its platform, which is mainly used to recruit employees or to publish news about the business.[28]

- Approximately 77% of Pinterest users are women.[29]

- LinkedIn is available in 25 languages.

---

24. Mary Bellis, "The History of Facebook and How It Was Invented," ThoughtCo, February 6, 2020, https://www.thoughtco.com/who-invented-facebook-1991791.

25. "35 Instagram Marketing Statistics - 2023 Update I 99Firms," n.d., https://99firms.com/blog/instagram-marketing-statistics/#gref.

26. More than one billion hours of videos are watched on YouTube every day.

27. "X (Formerly Twitter): Most-Followed Accounts Worldwide 2023 I Statista," Statista, August 25, 2023, https://www.statista.com/statistics/273172/twitter-accounts-with-the-most-followers-worldwide/.

28. Maddy Osman, "Mind-Blowing LinkedIn Statistics and Facts," Kinsta®, September 22, 2023, https://kinsta.com/blog/linkedin-statistics/.

29. Hannah Macready, "47 LinkedIn Statistics You Need To Know In 2023," Social Media Marketing & Management Dashboard, July 5, 2023, https://blog.hootsuite.com/linkedin-statistics-business/.

Quiz

1. **Which of the following is a key feature that differentiates social media from other**
   media?

   a. It creates customer satisfaction.

   b. It is used by marketers to create awareness about products.

   c. It is very expensive.

   d. It is useful for customer engagement.

2. **Which one of the following statements about social media is NOT true?**

   a. It is interactive.

   b. It has user-generated content.

   c. It makes use of Web 2.0 as a platform.

   d. Social media marketing is more expensive than traditional media.

3. **Created in 1997, _____ was the first social media platform.**

   a. Six Degrees

   b. Orkut

   c. Friendster

   d. Hi5

4. _____ is currently the most popular social media platform (in terms of users) among users and businesses alike.

    a. YouTube

    b. Instagram

    c. Facebook

    d. Twitter

5. Facebook is owned by _____.

    a. Meta Platforms

    b. Facebook Inc.

    c. Mark Zuckerberg

    d. Google

6. X (previously Twitter) has a character limit of _____.

    a. 120

    b. 140

    c. 240

    d. 280

7. **LinkedIn is a wholly-owned subsidiary of _____.**

    a. Facebook

    b. Google

    c. Microsoft

    d. Meta Platforms

8. **To compete with TikTok, YouTube came up with _____.**

    a. Reels

    b. Live Streams

    c. YouTube Shorts

    d. YouTube Reels

9. **Which country has the highest number of Facebook users?**

    a. USA

    b. India

    c. Indonesia

    d. China

10. Instagram offers a feature called _____, where you can invite up to 3 people to go live with together.

   a. Live Chats

   b. Live Streams

   c. Live

   d. Chat Rooms

Answers	1 − d	2 − d	3 − a	4 − c	5 − a
	6 − d	7 − c	8 − c	9 − b	10 − c

Chapter Summary

◆ Social media is a group of websites or web pages and applications that help users create content and share it.

◆ Social media is gaining momentum in countries all over the world, mainly due to the emergence of social media networks.

◆ Most of the traditional media are based on one-way communication. Social media, on the other hand, enables quick feedback and multi-way communication.

◆ Social media is a Web 2.0 application, consisting of user-generated content and having a high reach; it is highly interactive and easily accessible.

◆ With over 270 million social media users in the US (81% of its population) and 4.59 billion social media users in the world in 2022, social media has established itself globally and is growing rapidly.

◆ From the era where postal communication was the major mode of communication to today's modern-day world in which we communicate using computers and devices connected by the internet, the world of communication has come a long way.

◆ Six Degrees, created in 1997, was the first social media platform. Currently, there are thousands of social media sites, with over 30 of them having more than 100 million users.

◆ Facebook, YouTube, Instagram, Threads, Twitter, Pinterest, and LinkedIn are the major popular social media sites in the United States.

Chapter 2

Social Media Marketing

Social media marketing is emerging as a major marketing medium. Businesses across the world are adopting and effectively using social media to market their brands. This chapter explains the concept of social media marketing, its advantages and disadvantages. The chapter also discusses how social media marketing differs from traditional media. Further, we learn about organic vs. paid marketing and influencer marketing.

The key learning objectives should include the reader's understanding of the following:

- What is social media marketing?

- The advantages and disadvantages of social media marketing.

- How is social media marketing different from traditional media?

- What is organic versus paid marketing?

- What is influencer marketing?

- What is meant by communities?

- How to conduct competitor analysis using social media?

2.1 Social Media Marketing (SMM)

Our lives have become grossly dependent on social media. Whether we want to be in touch with our family and friends, read news about the world, voice our thoughts, or network with professionals in our field or just declare our love for puppies, social media furnishes us with everything. The revolutionary emergence of social media has given marketers a new and affordable avenue to market their products and services i.e., **Social Media Marketing (SMM).** The days of brick-and-mortar business are in the past. Businesses today need an online presence in the form of a website and social media accounts to make it easier for customers to find them without stepping out of their houses. Social media marketing is the use of social media sites to promote a company's products and services. Social media makes it easier for companies to advertise their products and services, announce offers, deals and discounts to quickly attract customers, and reply in real-time to grievances and feedback.

Social media is emerging as an important part of the media mix of companies. The goal of SMM is to produce content that users will share with their social network to help a company increase brand exposure and broaden customer reach.[30] Marketers are

---

30. Griffin LaFleur, "Social Media Marketing (SMM)," WhatIs.com, October 22, 2021, https://whatis.techtarget.com/definition/social-media-marketing-SMM.

using this tool to create a brand image, engage with customers, get feedback and reviews, answer customer queries, give product information, sell products, and create and increase brand awareness. Before social media came into the picture, a company's media mix consisted mainly of traditional media like television, newspapers, radio, hoardings, etc., and some amount of online advertising through emails, website banners, etc. But since its inception, social media has brought about a significant change in the media landscape.

With the smartphone boom and the 4G revolution by companies like Jio disrupting the market and getting other service providers to provide cheaper internet packages, the Indian market has seen a huge penetration in regard to social media. Almost every household has a smartphone now and most people use internet on their smartphones. This has made social media more accessible to all.

Social media marketing is being given more importance by marketers lately as it engages customers promptly, a feature that traditional media lacks. Social media requires the active involvement of users, which in turn, leads to deeper customer engagement as customers keep interacting with the brand through social media.

| Figure 2.1 | **Brand interaction via social media** |

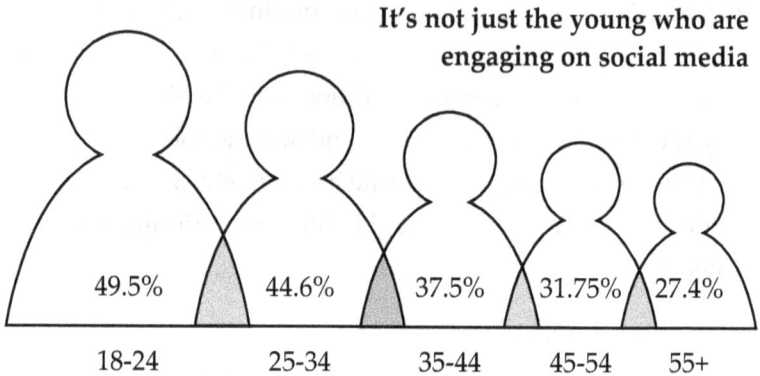

It's not just the young who are engaging on social media

| 49.5% | 44.6% | 37.5% | 31.75% | 27.4% |
| 18-24 | 25-34 | 35-44 | 45-54 | 55+ |

% of people from different age groups who have dealt with a brand through social media

Source: thenextweb.com Retrieved from: https://www.dbswebsite.com/blog/2017/01/24/growth-social-media-marketing-2017/

2.2 Importance and Scope of Social Media Marketing

Most companies in the world have a presence on Facebook and Twitter (X).[31] Facebook dominates the world as the social media site with the highest number of users. Exceptions are countries like Russia and China, which are dominated by other sites like VKontakte and Odnoklassniki (Russia), Sina Weibo and Qzone (China).

---

31. Neal Schaffer, "55 Compelling Social Media Marketing Statistics You Need To Know For 2024," Social Media & Influencer Marketing Speaker, Consultant & Author, October 27, 2023, https://nealschaffer.com/social-media-marketing-statistics/.

The United States is, by far, the largest social media advertising market in the world, as more than $72.3 billion was spent on social media ads in the country in 2023.[32] With high penetration, high engagement rate, and many other advantages (refer to 2.3.1 below), social media marketing is gaining massive momentum across the world.

With companies competing strongly to have an increased presence on social media, they are continuously seeking social media experts and there is a growing need for skilled personnel in the field. Companies are now seeking social media analysts, digital marketers, content managers, online community managers, public relations managers, social media specialists, and online influencers to name a few. With the predictions for its continued growth, social media marketing will be providing a huge number of career opportunities to youngsters who seek to pursue a career in this growing field.

The COVID-19 pandemic has increased the importance of social media enormously. A digital boom happened during the pandemic with more people going online to not just seek and search for brands, but purchase products too. Most businesses have gone digital to leverage the high number of social media users. Brands that were earlier not present on social media or had a limited presence are now adopting social media and increasing their social media presence to reach their target audience, penetrate into newer markets, engage with more customers, and create more buzz about their products.

Thus, we can see that globally, social media marketing is a fast-growing phenomenon, with most businesses having adopted

---

32. "Topic: Social Media Advertising and Marketing in the U.S.," Statista, August 31, 2023, https://www.statista.com/topics/8791/social-media-marketing-in-the-us/#topicOverview.

it in their marketing plan. Companies are spending more on social media marketing and these figures are expected to grow rapidly.

Brands like Nike[33], Starbucks[34], Dove[35], Oreo[36], Sephora[37], GoPro[38], Airbnb[39], and Netflix[40] have had the highest popularity in social media advertising. Many brands have followed suit by coming up with strong social media marketing campaigns.

---

33. Sweta Panigrahi, "Nike's Social Media Strategy: A Deep Dive into Campaigns & Statistics," Keyhole, August 18, 2023, https://keyhole.co/blog/nike-social-media-strategy/..

34. Kavya Ravi, "Starbucks' Social Media Strategy - What Brands Can Learn from Starbucks," Unmetric Social Media Analytics Blog, February 12, 2019, https://blog.unmetric.com/starbucks-social-media-strategy.

35. Malathi M. A. Sriram, "DOVE : Using Social Media for Social Viral Campaign - A Case Study." Shri Dharmasthala Manjunatheshwara Research Centre for Management Studies (SDM RCMS), SDMIMD, Mysore, Accessed June 06, 2023 : https://www.sdmimd.ac.in/SDMRCMS/cases/CIM2013/3.pdf.

36. "How Oreo's Adaptable Strategy Helps Them Dominate Social Media," https://www.insightsforprofessionals.com, n.d., https://www.insightsforprofessionals.com/marketing/social-media/how-oreo-dominates-social-media.

37. "Lessons from Sephora — Marketing Across Multiple Channels," n.d., https://www.responsival.com/post/lessons-from-sephora-marketing-across-multiple-channels..

38. Samuel Stroud, "GoPro Social Media: How Did It Become so Successful?," Giraffe Social - Social Media Agency, October 23, 2023, https://www.giraffesocialmedia.co.uk/gopro-social-media-how-did-it-become-so-successful/.

39. "Airbnb: Social Media Strategy - 1223 Words | Essay Example," IvyPanda, October 26, 2023, https://ivypanda.com/essays/airbnb-social-media-strategy/.

40. Sweta Panigrahi, "Netflix's Winning Social Media Strategy: A Deep Dive," Keyhole, April 6, 2023, https://keyhole.co/blog/netflixs-winning-social-media-strategy-a-deep-dive/#:~:text=Netflix's%20social%20media%20strategy%20involves,from%20their%20top%2Dperforming%20shows.

| Figure 2.2 | Dove's Partnership with Twitter for the #SpeakBeautiful Campaign |

#speak*beautiful*

The power is in our hands to make social media
a more positive place

Dove and Twitter: A partnership for social change

5⁺ million
negative beauty tweets
were sent by women
in 2014

4 out of every **5**
negative beauty tweets are
from women talking about
themselves

Your positive tweet can start a trend
Tweet one thing you love about yourself or a friend using #SpeakBeautiful

They would identify negative tweets about beauty and body image and respond to them in real-time while encouraging women to tweet about things they loved about themselves.

Figure 2.3   **Top social media platforms used by marketers worldwide (as of 2022)**

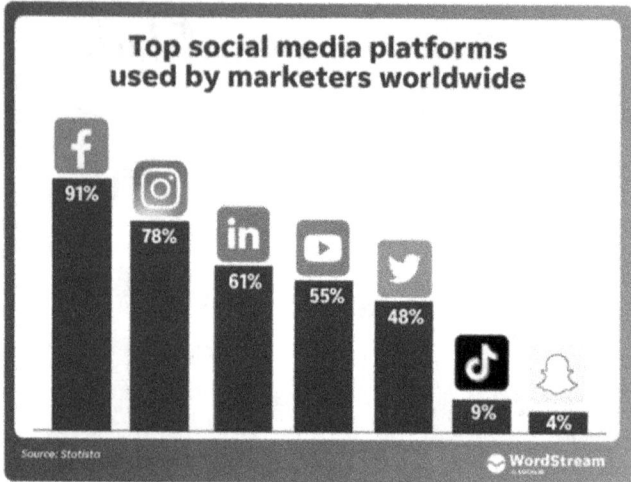

Source: https://www.wordstream.com/blog/ws/2022/01/11/most-popular-social-media-platforms

2.3 Advantages and Disadvantages of Social Media Marketing

The statistics shown in Fig 2.1 show how social media has grown and the massive reach it has amongst the world's internet population. But, it also has certain benefits and drawbacks that cannot be ignored.

2.3.1 Advantages of Social Media Marketing for businesses

1. **Less expensive**

   Social media marketing is less expensive compared to other

media like print and television. Running an advertising campaign on television, newspapers, radio, hoardings, and other traditional media incurs millions of dollars worth of advertising costs. Social media, on the other hand, is relatively cost-effective. You may need to hire and pay a social media marketing team to manage and run the social media accounts, but the costs are still relatively lower. Thus, the advertising cost is reduced for marketers. One of the metrics used for assessing SMM campaigns is Cost-Per-Thousand Impressions (CPM). The CPM of social media is less than $3 whereas the CPM for radio is around $10 and for TV, is a whopping $28.[41]

2. **Better customer engagement**
   Social media is a good platform for engaging with customers and getting first-hand feedback about the product, brand, company, and its services. Customers can like or dislike posts, leave comments, ask queries, and express grievances online, thus making it a good platform for the company to engage with customers and provide faster solutions to their problems. Hosting online events, free giveaways or even inviting customers and followers to write about their experience with your brand can make them feel a part of a community.

3. **Effective medium for targeting specific customer segments**
   Social media lets you select a specific target audience based on age, gender, location, and language, a feature that makes it a way better medium than traditional marketing channels. Targeted marketing helps you reach the right customers at the right time.

---

41. Lauren Tumminello, "Social Media ROI Case Study - AHBA | Firefly Marketing," Firefly Marketing (blog), June 2, 2023, https://marketwithfirefly.com/does-social-media-make-sense-for-my-roi/.

4. **Better customer satisfaction**

    Social media marketing helps in achieving better customer satisfaction. This is because the advertising reaches more of the desired target market who receive messages of their interest. Moreover, when businesses respond to customers' feedback, queries, and comments, they feel more connected to the brand which leads to increased satisfaction levels. For example, Imagine you buy a pair of headphones but realize that the product is defective. Instead of calling up customer care and going through a tedious replacement process, you can comment or directly message the company on social media. Companies readily solve customer complaints when the complaint is visible to their other followers to avoid building a negative image. This leads to greater customer satisfaction too! Similarly, after buying a product, if you see positive reinforcement messages on the brand's social media page, it leads to increased satisfaction as you are reassured that you have made the right decision by purchasing the said product.

5. **Increased brand awareness**

    With more and more people using social media, users are exposed to various brands. If the company shares interesting content such as witty or engaging advertisements or brand information, users will become aware of the brand and its offerings. This in turn ignites a desire in them to know more about and even purchase the brand's products.

6. **More inbound traffic**

    Social media marketing helps reach customers even before they buy the products. When they view the products' ads on social media pages, they come to know about them and may remember them when they decide to shop. Most of the customers who see a product online may like it (or like the brand that offers it), visit the product page, or be redirected to the company website. This increases the inbound traffic to the brand page and website and the interested user may get converted into a customer.

2.3.2 Disadvantages of Social Media Marketing

While the advantages of social media certainly outweigh its disadvantages, the disadvantages shouldn't be ignored. Some disadvantages are as follows:

1. **Time-consuming process**
    You must continuously post updates and reply to users who have posted comments, queries, or feedback. All this requires dedication and time. You may need a dedicated social media manager to manage your social media accounts, respond in real-time to users, post regular updates, and measure effectiveness. Small businesses with a small team may not be able to dedicate as much time as social media marketing requires.

2. **Requires skilled personnel**
    You require skilled personnel to handle your social media marketing. Depending on the size of the business, a single person or an entire team of social media experts would be required. They must be qualified to design and create social media accounts, manage traffic, respond to comments, queries, and feedback in an effective manner, run social media advertising campaigns, conduct research about

competitors' social media activity, stay updated with the latest trends and technology and evaluate and control the effectiveness of social media marketing campaigns.

3. **Risk of negative comments**

   There is a risk of negative comments and spam messages by disgruntled users, which, when read by prospective customers or others, may have a negative impact on the brand image which in turn might negatively influence their purchase decision. Sometimes there may be fake negative comments by trolls or competitors. This negativity can affect the brand image and make you lose prospective customers.

4. **Exposure to competitors**

   When you use social media marketing, it is inevitable that everyone can see your content. This includes competitors who may see and learn from what you are doing and replicate it. They may be able to get better insights into your marketing strategy. This, however, is beyond your control, and hence most businesses seek to ignore this disadvantage as there isn't much they can do about it.

5. **Reach is limited to the technologically literate**

   Social media marketing does not reach illiterate people, nor is it reachable to those who are not using the internet, or do not own a personal computer or a smartphone. Though more and more people are using social media, almost half of the world's population does not have an online presence. If your target market includes such people, social media is not suitable for you. For example, a company selling uniforms to underprivileged school kids in villages with no internet access will not be able to market to the kids using social media, or a company selling hearing aids to the elderly may not be able to effectively reach older people who are technologically illiterate or have limited access to the technology required for social media.

2.4 Traditional Media vs. Social Media

Television, radio, newspapers, magazines, hoardings, posters, banners, online media which include websites, banners on websites, search engine results, email, online classified advertisements, pop-up advertisements, etc., and social media are the major media that marketers use in their media mix. Of these, barring online and social media, they are all known as traditional media. Traditional media and social media are different in the following ways:

Table 2.1	Differences between traditional media and social media	
Sr. No.	**Traditional Media**	**Social Media**
1.	**Based on one-way communication** If a marketer shows an advertisement on television, he has no way of knowing whether the viewer likes it or not, or when a reader sees an advertisement in the newspaper, the marketer doesn't get his feedback. In fact, there is no way of knowing how many people actually saw the advertisement.	**Includes two-way or multi-way communication** But on social media, users may like the ad, click on the website link, post comments, or share the ad. Even the number of views can be counted. Marketers can even respond to the comments and other users, too, may comment on other users' posts.
2.	**Traditional media does not provide customer engagement.** If a customer likes a TV advertisement or newspaper advertisement, he cannot provide instant feedback or query to the marketer nor can the marketer address the audience's queries.	**Social media provides customer engagement.** If a customer has liked a product he may comment on the social media page about his good experience. The company can, then, thank him for his positive review, inform him of any promotional offers or remind him to purchase more. This interaction may be seen by other prospective customers who wish to buy, and their purchase decision may be reinforced.

Sr. No.	Traditional Media	Social Media
3.	**Traditional media is relatively more expensive than social media.**	**Social media is relatively cheaper than traditional media.**
	The cost of advertising on television is very high. The average cost to run a 30-second television commercial on a national network is $104,700*. The marketer also needs to plan for production expenses for the television advertisement which may cost anything between $1,000 to $50,000.[42]	In comparison, social media is relatively cheaper. Companies can create and manage their social media pages in-house or through social media agencies which may charge some fees. Social media advertisements cost as little as $7-$30 for 1000 impressions. This means that a company may spend anything from approximately $7 to $30 to reach 1000 people or for 1000 people to view the social media ad. This concept is known as CPM which stands for Cost per Thousand.
	Similarly, advertising in newspapers, magazines, hoardings, or the radio are expensive affairs. They include printing or publishing costs, production costs, purchase of advertising space, and payment to advertising agencies or professionals.	Companies can also run ads using CPC (Cost per Click) which may range from less than a dollar to $4. CPC is the cost incurred by the company for each click on their advertisement.

42. Elizabeth Kraus and Audrey Rawnie Rico, "Everything You Need to Know about TV Advertising Costs," Fit Small Business (blog), March 14, 2023, https://fitsmallbusiness.com/tv-advertising/.

Sr. No.	Traditional Media	Social Media
4	**Customers trust traditional media more than social media.**	**Social media marketing is more effective in creating brand loyalty.**
	A newspaper advertisement or paid article holds more credibility than a social media ad or a blog shared on social media, because it is tangible, can be held, and hence readers perceive it more positively.	Studies have shown that a positive interaction with a brand on social media increases the brand image among customers, leading to loyalty towards the brand.
5.	**Traditional media, due to its wider reach, can be used to market to the mass market.**	**Social media can be used to reach more niche and targeted audiences.**
	As most people own a television set, subscribe to and read newspapers, see hoardings, and listen to the radio, a mass market can be covered using these traditional media.	If a brand wants to reach travel enthusiasts, it can advertise on travel-based social media groups.

2.5 Social Media vs. Traditional Media as Parts of the Media Mix

To understand what media mix is, we need to delve into the promotion mix of a company. The promotion mix of a company is also known as its communication mix. It consists of advertising, personal selling, direct marketing, and sales promotion. The company uses its desired mix of the above elements of the promotion mix in its communication program, known as Integrated Marketing Communications.

Marketing communications have been defined by Kevin Keller[43] as "the means by which firms attempt to inform, persuade, and remind consumers–directly or indirectly–about the products and brands they sell." The advent of new communication technologies has given companies access to new media to interact with existing and targeted customers. Consumers have better control over what messages they wish to receive and when too.

Advertising is an important element of the promotion mix. Kotler and Keller have defined advertising as "any paid form of non-personal presentation and promotion of ideas, goods, or services by an identified sponsor."[44]

Advertising is done using channels of communication. There are two types of channels–personal and non-personal. Channels of communication are also known as media of communication or advertising media. Personal forms of communication channels or media include phone calls, emails, word-of-mouth recommendations, etc. Non-personal channels include media that carry the advertising message without personal contact or feedback. Major media include print media like newspapers, magazines, pamphlets, brochures, catalogs, etc.; broadcast media like television, radio, etc.; display media like hoardings, banners, posters, etc.; and online media like company websites, and social media.

---

43. Philip Kotler et al., Marketing Management: A South Asian Perspectives, 14th Edition, Pearson Prentice Hall eBooks, 2009, https://repository.iimb.ac.in/handle/2074/12402.

44. Ibid.

Each of these media comes with its own set of benefits and limitations. You must select the media you want to use based on various factors.

With such a wide variety of media channels available for advertisers/companies, media strategy, and media planning have evolved into important functions for advertising managers. One of the most important tasks in the overall integrated marketing communications program is to prepare an effective media strategy. Media strategy is the process of analyzing and choosing media for advertising and promotion campaigns.[45]

Media strategy is considered an important area for media managers or marketers, as once you decide on your media strategy, other aspects of media planning can be put into action.

Media planning is a function that helps determine the most effective manner of spending the advertiser's money across media to generate the best return on the investment for the brand.[46]

Media planning helps you decide:

1. Which media should be selected for various promotional objectives or marketing messages?

2. How much money should be spent on which media?

3. When should the particular media be used?

Media planning has evolved into a crucial function in marketing with companies choosing to either use in-house media planners or external agencies that offer specialized media

45. Kenneth E. Clow and Donald Baack, Integrated Advertising, Promotion & Marketing Communications, 2004, http://ci.nii.ac.jp/ncid/BA68680727.

46. K. Shah, A. D'Souza, 2009, Advertising and Promotion- An IMC Perspective, Tata McGraw Hill, New Delhi.

planning services. The advertising message, once developed, needs to reach the right kind of audience and have the desired impact. It is important to select the right media for communicating a particular message Thus, the primary function of media planners is to decide where and when to place advertisements.

A company wishing to advertise its product(s) must focus on media selection. You must carefully evaluate various media available, their advantages and disadvantages or limitations, along with the budget, objectives, reach of the media, etc.

A media mix is a blend of different media that will be used to effectively reach the target audience. Gartner[47] has defined media mix as "A media mix is the blend of paid communication channels that an organization uses to get its messaging and brand across to potential customers. A media mix typically includes social media, traditional print ads, TV ads, and direct email."

You may use a concentrated or assorted media mix. A concentrated media mix means investing the entire media budget in one medium, which gives you control and a greater impact on a specific target audience. It offers a number of benefits to the marketers. Firstly, it helps you become more dominant as compared to your competitors in a particular medium. Secondly, if a concentrated media mix is used to select high-visibility media, such as prime-time television or popular magazines, you may gain preferential treatment from distributors and retailers as it can create enthusiasm and loyalty among them, thus earning you a better shelf space or inventory. Thirdly, among target customers having limited media exposure, a concentrated media mix may create brand awareness and familiarity with the brand. Lastly,

---

47. "Definition of Media Mix - Gartner Marketing Glossary," Gartner, n.d., https://www.gartner.com/en/marketing/glossary/media-mix#:~:text=A%20media%20mix%20is%20the,TV%20ads%20and%20direct%20email.

significant investment in a single kind of media may help you get discounts from media organizations.

An assorted media mix makes use of a variety of media to reach target audiences. By using an assorted media mix, you can place different advertisements in different media, thus, reaching different target audiences. Using an assorted media mix has many benefits. Messages can be tailored to each target audience group's unique requirements, thus enabling you to reach different target audiences. It helps in increasing the reach of a message as compared to a single medium. The probability of reaching target audiences exposed to a variety of media is more when multiple media are used. If the target customer receives different messages via different media, the learning effect may be enhanced and the effectiveness of the message may be better.

Once you select the media, the next step is to decide the combination of the media mix to be used. This will be decided by considering your marketing objectives, target market, market characteristics, and matching with the target market.[48]

A study by Chattopadhyay et al.[49] has shown that as a consumer gains more knowledge about a product category, he starts behaving differently from first-time buyers, who have less knowledge about the category. This shows that an assorted media mix influences buyer behavior by increasing their information or knowledge about the product.

---

48. S. A. Chunawalla, K. C. Sethia, 2008, Foundations of Advertising, Mumbai, Himalaya Publishing House.

49. Tanmay Chattopadhyay, Rudrendu Narayan Dutta, and Shradha Sivani, "Media Mix Elements Affecting Brand Equity: A Study of the Indian Passenger Car Market," IIMB Management Review 22, no. 4 (December 1, 2010): 173–85, https://doi.org/10.1016/j.iimb.2010.09.001.

2.6 Organic Versus Paid Marketing

In simple words, organic marketing is marketing you don't pay for. Organic marketing includes the content you post on your social media page that doesn't have any budget behind it. For example, you write a post or upload a video to your social media page and wait for the audience to see it on their feed. Organic content is posted for free. Organic marketing is used for creating and sustaining the community of followers that develops around your brand. It helps to offer content that can increase leads as well as sales, and retain existing customers.

But, when should you use organic marketing? When you aim to reach existing customers who are following you on social media, organic marketing is the best option. You can update your social media posts, share new content, engage with existing customers, and target potential customers who may visit your social media page.

Paid marketing, on the other hand, has a budget behind it. Paid posts reach a larger audience as you pay for them to reach people other than your followers. Paid posts have a sponsored tag on them. These are posts, videos, and other content that you need to pay for in order for it to reach the audience. They will show up on the feed of whichever audience you decide to target with your content or ad. They generally use Cost per Click (CPC) or Cost per Thousand Impressions (CPM) as a method of advertising. Paid marketing should be used when you want to reach a larger audience and want guaranteed, quick results.

You can combine your organic posts with paid marketing by for example, clicking on the boost post button on Facebook. This will take your organic posts to your desired audience at a lower price. Comparatively, paid marketing will cost you more but also provides you with more options like more refined targeting and a much larger reach. It also helps to increase your brand awareness, generate more website traffic, and drive your sales.

The same content can be organic or paid depending on the way it is shared. For example, if you share a reel marketing women's formal wear on your Facebook page, it is organic marketing and will only be visible to your followers, page visitors, and friends of your followers who share this reel on their timeline. If you pay Facebook to show this reel to your target audience and the reel appears to all women who have searched for formal wear recently or bought women's formal wear in the past, it is paid marketing.

Similarly, you may post a pre-produced video highlighting the features of your new microwave oven on your YouTube channel. This is organic marketing as you are not paying YouTube to showcase this video to your target audience. If you pay YouTube, and the same video shows up in the form of an ad when users are watching other content on YouTube, it is paid marketing.

Figure 2.4	Organic vs. Paid (Sponsored) Posts

Organic Post	Sponsored Post

Benefits of Organic Marketing

1. You can build customer relationships by engaging with them— regularly posting, replying to their comments, answering queries, redressing grievances, and providing customer support.

2. As all your posts will show up on your followers' feeds, you can build brand awareness.

3. You can remind customers about your brand so that you stay relevant in their memory when they think of making a purchase.

4. It is free and therefore, very useful for people with small businesses and limited marketing budgets.

5. It has a longer life as posts last forever unless you delete them.

6. It is useful to convey additional information that is not covered by your ads, such as latest updates, upcoming offers, product changes, price changes, website or blog links, etc.

Limitations of Organic Marketing

1. Results may take time as you may not reach your target audience and even when you do, they may not need your product immediately. Those who do may not be your followers, and thus may not see your posts when they are making their purchase decision.

2. It is visible only to your followers or page visitors.

3. The continuously changing algorithms of social media pages make it more difficult for your posts to show up on your followers' feeds.

4. It is time-consuming as you need to ensure continuous engagement with your followers.

5. Organic marketing is not targeted. You cannot target the audience based on their search or purchase intention and must instead create a post that is relevant to most or all of your followers.

Benefits of Paid Marketing

1. It helps you boost organic marketing posts that are doing well.

2. You can target a specific audience and reach new audiences. You can also customize ads for different audiences.

3. You can choose from a variety of ad formats such as images, videos, carousel ads, collection ads, canvas ads, story ads, etc

4. It increases website traffic conversions and generates leads.

5. Using analytics, you can measure the effectiveness of various ad campaigns.

6. It is cost-effective as it results in faster revenue growth.

7. It gives faster results as the ad is shown to people looking for similar products.

Limitation of Paid Marketing

1. You need to continuously monitor paid ads to ensure you are getting the desired results, and re-evaluate your strategy accordingly.

2. It is highly competitive as many brands are bidding for ad space.

3. It may be expensive for small businesses or if you have a limited marketing budget.

4. Requires a skilled social media manager or a team to run the various types of ads, monitor and alter them based on trends.

5. The audience may find the ads disruptive, repetitive or annoying.

2.7 Influencer Marketing

Any talk of social media marketing is incomplete without the mention of influencers. Social media influencers are people who collaborate with brands to promote their products and services on social media platforms. An influencer is a person who has the power to influence the buying decisions of others because of his/ her knowledge, expertise, or relationship with the audience. Many years back, the influencer market was limited to celebrities and models. Now there are many social media users who have become social media influencers in various spheres such as travel, food, fashion, cosmetics, electronics, etc.

Influencer marketing works because users trust social media influencers; they are considered experts whose opinions are valued by their followers. Their recommendations work like word-of-mouth testimonials for your brands. Following are some of the goals you can achieve using influencer marketing:

- Create brand awareness

- Increase sales

- Increase your number of followers

- Attract a new market

- Retain customers

A study of over 2000 Americans conducted by Morning Consult[50] found that almost 75% of Gen Z and millennials follow influencers on social media. The study further found that a majority of them most often learn about new products they're interested in via social media. Thus, by leveraging influencers, you can easily reach young Americans. For this purpose, you just need to adequately understand how and where to engage them.

Influencers can be classified into four types based on the number of followers they have:

1. Mega influencers have more than one million followers. These are generally actors, activists, athletes, sportspersons, musicians, artists, or other public figures. Examples of mega influencers include:

   - Roger Federer who has over 11 million followers on Instagram and over 12 million on Twitter.

   - J.K. Rowling who has over 14 million followers on Instagram.

   - Indian cricketer Virat Kohli who has over 250 million followers on Instagram and over 55 million on Twitter.

   - Priyanka Chopra Jonas who has over 87 million followers on Instagram and over three million followers on Twitter.

Mega influencers can be beneficial for high-end luxury brands, large enterprises, or brands targeting a broad target market.

---

50. Morning Consult Staff, "The Influencer Report," Morning Consult Pro, September 26, 2023, https://pro.morningconsult.com/analyst-reports/influencer-report.

2. Macro influencers are those with 100,000 to one million followers. They are generally people with authority in their chosen area and have a wider reach than micro influencers. But their engagement rates are lower than micro influencers. Engagement rate means the number of engagements generated by the followers in terms of likes, shares, comments, etc. Examples of macro influencers include:

- Influencers with more than 800k followers on Instagram, Amy Jackson (fashion_jackson) is a macro influencer who posts on topics related to fashion, travel, and lifestyle.

- Ashley Galvin is a US-based yoga instructor who has over 500k followers on Instagram.

- Renee Chow is a beauty influencer with over 600K subscribers on her YouTube channel and over 200k followers on Instagram.

3. Micro influencers have 10,000 to 100,000 followers. Though their reach is limited as compared to macro and mega influencers, they have a high engagement rate and capture a more niche, highly targeted audience. They are readily available for the marketers as well as the audience and are generally more cost-effective than macro and mega influencers, which makes them popular among marketers. Following are a few examples of micro influencers:

- Chelsea Martin is a travel influencer who has over 25k followers on Instagram. Her posts have high engagement rates and she usually writes about personalized luxury travel, making her a good choice for luxury hotels, resorts, and travel companies.

- Marie Denee is a fashion influencer. Her page is called "The Curvy Fashionista" and has over 60k followers.

- Elizabeth Moye's page "Hello Spoonful" has over 74k followers. She is a nutritionist who shares healthy recipes.

4. Nano influencers have less than 10,000 followers. Despite having a low reach, they have a very strong connection with the audience due to more personal and relatable interactions with their followers. They are much more cost-effective than mega, macro, and micro influencers and are suitable for businesses wishing to reach a more niche target audience–specific communities and demographics. Here are a few examples of nano influencers:

- Alexis Baker is a beauty influencer who has worked with well-known beauty, clothing, and skincare brands. She has over 4000 Instagram followers and over 300 subscribers on YouTube.

- Noelle Graham has over 8500 followers and blogs on various topics related to motherhood, fashion, and art.

- Filip Cromade has over 6000 followers. He is a male fashion influencer.

Figure 2.5 **Limitations of paid marketing**

Mega Influencers

- More than 1 Million Followers

Macro Influencers

- 100k to 1 Million Followers

Micro Influencers

- 10k to 100k Followers

Nano Influencers

- Less than 10k Followers

If you're looking to partner with influencers for your brand, you must search for the ones that would be the right fit for your brand. If you're looking for a broader target audience spread across various demographics, you may choose macro or mega influencers. If you're looking at a more niche, more engaged, and highly targeted audience, then you can select micro or nano influencers. Your budget, too, would play a vital role in the selection of influencers. The more followers an influencer has, the higher they will charge for sponsored posts or endorsements.

Tips for creating an influencer marketing strategy:

- Choose your target audience and social media platform.

- Determine your influencer marketing budget.

- Search for influencers. You can use an influencer marketing agency too. Check their followers, engagement rates, and marketing costs.

- Set your campaign goals and message.

- Choose the right influencer by seeing if they fit with your goals and are relevant to your target audience.

- Analyze and evaluate your influencer marketing campaign.

Tips for promoting your influencer marketing strategy:

- Send free samples or products to influencers that you want to market your product.

- Partner with influencers to offer discount codes for your products to their followers.

- Pay for sponsored posts and recommendations.

- Work across different social media platforms, with different influencers if necessary.

- Allow influencers to use their creativity to create and share content by clicking pictures and shooting videos.

2.8 Competitor Analysis Using Social Media

Today's business world has numerous players. If a customer wants to buy a particular product, there are hundreds of options to select from, i.e., a customer is spoilt for choice. Hence it becomes imperative that you know who your competitors are, what they are doing, and what their future plans are. Competitor analysis helps in understanding the competitors' strategies and using this information for formulating your business strategies. A business needs to follow what its competitors are doing on social media, how they are using social media, what offers they are running, and how they are engaging customers. Social media competitor analysis can be defined as the process of evaluating your competitors on social media to find opportunities and accordingly building strategies for brand growth.[51]

2.8.1 Identification of keywords and competitors

You should prepare a keyword inventory that will help you identify the key players in the market who would be your major competitors. For example, if a restaurant wants to do a competitive analysis, the keywords could be: best restaurants in San Jose, best Indian Cuisine Restaurants in San Jose, best places to eat in San Jose, etc. Through these keywords, a search can be performed on Google or on various social media platforms, which will help you understand which are the major players in that segment, i.e., who are your competitors. Google AdWords Keyword Planner is one of the tools that can be used to identify keywords easily. You should also learn which social platforms

51. Ofuonyebi, Sally. "Social Media Competitor Analysis: The Complete Guide." Moz, July 27, 2022. https://moz.com/blog/social-media-competitor-analysis. .

your competitors use, how actively they use them, and what their marketing strategies are.

2. Collecting data

Once you have identified and narrowed down your key competitors, you must conduct a search to find out the following information related to your competitors:

- Which social media platforms are they on?

- How many followers do they have?

- Who are their top followers?

- What content are they using?

- How often are they sharing new content?

- What is their engagement rate?

- How many messages are they sending and receiving?

- Which hashtags are they using most often and how many hashtags are they using?

- What is their share of voice? (Share of voice: Share of voice represents how much people are talking about a particular brand on social media as compared to the total mentions for all brands in the industry)

- How many followers are they gaining/losing over a period of time (say 30 days)?

- Which are their top posts?

You can visit the competitors' websites, conduct a quick search online, or use various social media marketing and competitive research tools to find and collect this information.

3. Analyzing data

Once all the required data is collected, you must analyze this data to be able to make sense of it and use it productively in framing your own social media marketing strategies. SWOT Analysis can be done to identify the Strengths, Weaknesses, Opportunities, and Threats faced by each competitor and these can be used to compare with the business's own SWOTs. There are also many tools for conducting a social media competitive analysis, such as Brandwatch, Not Just Analytics (formerly Ninjalistics), Sprout Social, Phlanx, FollowerWonk, Socialbakers, SocialMention, BigSpy, Sparktoro, Sociality.io, and many more.

The analysis will help you identify how active your competitors are on social media, the kind of content they publish, and the frequency and popularity of their posts. You can then use this information to formulate your own strategies.

4. Formulating a social media marketing strategy

Once the analysis has revealed the answers to all the questions and revealed the marketing strategies of competitors, you can identify which areas they are lacking in, which parts they can improve, what they're doing better, or what you can do better than competitors. Basically, the analysis can be used as a benchmark to design your social media strategies and activities. You can make any changes to your existing strategy based on the findings. The competitive analysis also helps identify the latest trends in the industry which can be implemented into your business's social media marketing plan.

Exercise:

Evaluate the traditional media advertisements as well as social media advertisements of any 10 brands of your choice. Note the differences, namely the duration, content, message, mode of communication (pictures, videos, audio, etc.), and discuss which ones are better and more effective and why.

Quiz

1. **Which media provides two-way and multi-way communication to marketers and the audience?**

   a. Television

   b. Radio

   c. Social media

   d. Hoardings

2. **Which one of the following statements related to social media marketing is NOT true?**

   a. Social media marketing is less expensive than traditional media.

   b. It is less trusted compared to traditional media.

   c. Traditional media has a wider reach than social media marketing.

   d. Social media marketing is less effective in customer engagement than traditional media.

3. _____ is defined in terms of "active involvement," and it can lead to "deep commitment" through the customer's progressive investments in the relationship.

    a. Customer engagement

    b. Customer satisfaction

    c. Customer loyalty

    d. Customer retention

4. Marketers are making use of social media marketing for the following reason(s)–

    a. to engage with customers

    b. to create a brand image

    c. to get feedback and reviews

    d. to increase brand awareness

    e. All of the above

5. Which age group has dealt the most with a brand on social media?

    a. 18-34

    b. 13-18

    c. 35-54

    d. 55+

6. **Social media pages linked to company websites lead to conversion into sales.**

   a. True

   b. False

7. **Most companies in English-speaking countries in the world have a presence on Facebook and Twitter.**

   a. True

   b. False

8. **_____ is, by far, the largest social media advertising market in the world.**

   a. India

   b. China

   c. US

   d. Brazil

9. **Which country has the highest number of Facebook users?**

   a. US

   b. India

   c. Indonesia

   d. China

10. The COVID-19 pandemic has increased the importance of social media enormously.

   a. True

   b. False

Answers	1 − c	2 − d	3 − a	4 − e	5 − a
	6 − a	7 − a	8 − c	9 − b	10 − a

Chapter Summary

◆ Social media marketing is the marketing of products or brands using social media platforms or social networking sites.

◆ Social media is emerging as an important element of the media mix of companies alongside traditional media like television, newspapers, radio, films, hoardings, transit advertisements, etc.

◆ The US is the largest market in the world for social media marketing.

◆ A whopping 92% of marketers in companies with more than 100 employees were expected to use social media marketing by 2021.

◆ With high penetration, high engagement rate, and many other advantages, social media marketing is gaining massive momentum across the world.

◆ Companies are spending more and more on social media marketing.

◆ The importance of social media has increased post the pandemic and the digital revolution.

◆ Traditional media, although it has a good reach, is based on one-way communication. Social media, on the other hand, enables quick feedback, customer engagement, and two and multi-way communication.

◆ The pros of social media marketing are that it is less expensive, more engaging, can target specific market segments more effectively, increases website traffic, and also results in better customer satisfaction. On the other hand, it has a few cons too. It is time-consuming, not favorable for those lacking computer literacy, is open to negative comments by others which is mostly out in the open for all to see, and is easily accessible by competitors.

This page is intentionally left blank

Chapter **3**

Social Media Marketing Strategies

This chapter delves into an extremely important part of social media marketing — social media marketing strategies. It talks about social media marketing plans versus strategies and takes the reader into the marketing planning process. Readers can get valuable insights about framing social media marketing strategies including how to set objectives; identify and understand the target audience; and create social media mission statements, schedules, and calendars. Readers will also learn how to use various metrics and social media management tools and analyze their marketing strategies.

> The key learning objectives should include understanding of the following points:
>
> - Meaning of social media marketing strategy
>
> - Social Media Marketing Plan: Meaning, Contents, and Process of Marketing Plan
>
> - Designing social media marketing strategies

A social media strategy is a plan that outlines your social media goals, the tactics used to achieve them, and metrics tracked to measure performance.[52] A social media marketing strategy summarizes everything that a business plans to do, i.e., all the actions it plans to take to achieve its objectives on social media.

A social media strategy acts like a detailed blueprint that answers all the questions you may have related to the content you post on your social media pages. It contains a well-thought-out plan, ideas, objectives, and the path to achieve those objectives. You must start designing your social media marketing strategy well before creating your content. A social media marketing strategy is a key ingredient of the social media marketing of a company. It helps to understand the target audience, their needs and wants, align those needs with the business's goals, and attract customers with offers designed for them.

While designing a social media marketing strategy, you must answer the following questions:

- Who is your audience? What are they looking for?

---

52. Clodagh O'Brien, "How to Develop a Social Media Strategy That Drives Brand Awareness & ROI," Digital Marketing Institute, July 3, 2023, https://digitalmarketinginstitute.com/blog/social-media-strategy.

- What kind of content should you create and share?

- How should your brand be perceived?

- Which social media platforms should you use?

- What goals and objectives do you wish to achieve?

You may have multiple social media goals. You can use a single or a mix of social media platforms to achieve those goals. Your goals may include generating more leads, creating a brand image, sharing product or service information, increasing brand awareness, increasing sales and market share, etc.

Additionally, you can also build different strategies for different social media platforms, depending on the nature of the platform and its demographics. For example, you can use Facebook to generate new leads, Instagram to share images and reels, Twitter to share product features, and YouTube to post informational videos.

3.1 Plan vs. Strategy

Many times, we talk about plans and strategies as if they're the same. *While a plan tells us what to do, a strategy tells us how to do it.* Basically, a plan is a statement of purpose regarding what action needs to be taken to achieve a goal or objective. A strategy, on the other hand, underlines how best to achieve that plan. For example, a company may have the following plan: To increase sales by 20% in the next financial quarter. It can adopt different strategies to achieve this plan. For instance, it may decide to run a sales promotion program and offer free gifts or discounts on products to boost sales. Or it may have a strategy to advertise the product strongly on social media, providing links to buy the product. Alternatively, it may give more margins to retailers to push the product into the market, or it can change the price of the product. So, while the plan is to increase sales, the company can adopt different strategies to achieve that plan. Thus, plans and strategies are closely related.

3.2 Social Media Marketing Plan

Companies use social media marketing to meet their marketing objectives. Whenever objectives need to be achieved, there is a need for proper planning. Marketers must design a good social media marketing plan which will help them achieve their objectives. Planning also lays the base for control so that you can deal with any contingencies and check whether things are going as planned or if there are any changes required.

A social media marketing plan is a part or an extension of a company's marketing plan. Marketing planning can be defined as the structured process of researching and analyzing marketing situations; developing and documenting marketing objectives, strategies, and programs; and implementing, evaluating, and controlling activities to achieve goals.[53]

Taking this definition forward, we can say that social media marketing planning is the structured process of researching and analyzing social media marketing situations; developing and documenting social media marketing objectives, strategies, and

---

53. Marc Oliver Opresnik, "Effective Social Media Marketing Planning – How to Develop a Digital Marketing Plan," in Lecture Notes in Computer Science, 2018, https://doi.org/10.1007/978-3-319-91521-0_24.

programs; and implementing, evaluating, and controlling social media marketing activities to achieve social media marketing goals.

With the help of a social media marketing plan, you can determine your target audience, which social networks to join, as well as the type of content you need to develop and share with your target audience. Thus, a social media marketing plan is a vital part of a business' overall marketing strategy.

You must design a good social media marketing plan that is clear, concise, measurable, controllable, flexible, and easy to implement and evaluate. This will help you in implementing various social media tasks and checking their progress to ensure that objectives are being achieved.

What does a social media marketing plan include?

Figure 3.1 Contents of a social media marketing plan

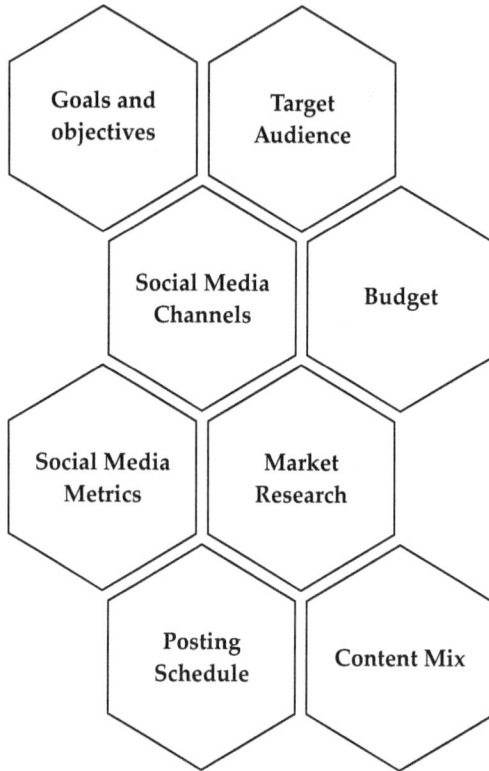

1. Goals and objectives

A social media plan must begin by defining the goals and objectives that you aim to achieve through social media marketing activities. Having clear goals and objectives helps in proper planning by understanding what needs to be done to achieve those goals and objectives. They help in setting a direction in which you can work and help coordinate and integrate the efforts of all team members in that common direction. Many people use the words goals and objectives interchangeably; however, they are different. A goal is an outcome that one wishes to achieve; it is a statement about the future of the business. Objectives, on the other hand, are specific actions and measurable tasks or actions taken to achieve those goals. While goals may be general, intangible, and immeasurable, objectives are more specific, tangible, and measurable. For example, a business's goal could be to provide excellent delivery whereas the objective to achieve this goal would be to deliver the product within 24 hours. So, for designing a social media plan, you must define your goals and objectives clearly.

2. Target audience

The next component of a social media plan is the target audience. Understanding one's target audience is especially important as it helps to plan according to the kind of audience, their tastes, habits, preferences, behavior, needs and wants, and fulfilling them by providing value and satisfaction through goods and services. A social media marketing plan can be designed to target a specific audience by understanding their needs clearly.

3. Social media channels

The next component of a social media marketing plan is the social media channel(s) you need to use. Once you identify and understand your target audience, you can select the social media sites best suited for those audiences and use them effectively. Different social media platforms have audiences with different demographics. The choice of social media marketing channels is important as companies can then design advertisements and content accordingly. For example: videos for YouTube, Reels for Instagram, Posts for Facebook, Tweets for Twitter, and so on.

For example, if a business finds that its target audience is active on Twitter, it may have to plan marketing activities, including relevant, effective content like what to tweet, when and how often to tweet, and also design ads for Twitter that will reach the target audience.

4. Social media metrics

You must be able to use the right kind of metrics to measure whether your social media marketing plan is effective. Metrics help in understanding the impact and effectiveness of a social media marketing plan on your revenues and marketing efforts, identify whether what you are doing is right or if you need to make changes in your marketing campaigns, and gauge how well your social media marketing plan is working. You can use metrics such as:

- Reach

- Impressions

- Response rate

- Click-through rate

- Return on investment

- Generated traffic

You can use tools such as Google Analytics to track these metrics.

5. Social media marketing budget

A social media marketing budget is the percentage of the marketing budget that will be devoted to social media. Basically, it is a document specifying how much you will spend on social media marketing activities over a specific period of time. Most companies spend between $200 and $350 per day, i.e., between $6000 and $10500 a month on social media marketing.[54]

In a survey conducted in March 2023, responding marketers in the United States indicated that 17% of their marketing budget was devoted to social media marketing.[55] This means that if a company has a marketing budget of $100,000 for a particular period, its social media marketing budget would be approximately $17000 for the given period.

The budget helps to measure the expected and actual rate of return on investments and keep a check on expenditure.

6. Market research

You need to understand the market where you plan to sell your products and services. Market research helps you gain a better understanding and clarity about the market, customers, consumer behavior, demographics, seasonality, social media sites, social media marketing trends, target audience, their behavior and preferences, etc.

Through market research, you can also gain insights into competitor activities, strategies, and industry trends. You can gather customer data such as their shopping habits, purchasing power, social media usage, online behavior, lifestyle preferences, brand attitudes, and a lot more. Companies such as Facebook provide such data to advertisers who use this data, in turn, to

---

54. Evolve, "How Much Should I Spend On Social Media Marketing?," Evolve Media, September 21, 2022, https://evolvemedia.com/how-much-should-i-spend-on-social-media-marketing/.

55. Statista, "U.S. Businesses Social Media Marketing Budget Share 2015-2024," July 4, 2023, https://www.statista.com/statistics/1223663/social-media-marketing-budget-share-usa/.

advertise more effectively.

7. Content mix and posting schedule

Content is the life of all social media marketing plans. Deciding on the right mix of content is an important element of the social media marketing plan. What part of the content should be informative, how much of the content should focus on sales promotion, and how much of it should focus on educating or entertaining the audience needs to be decided by you.

3.3 Process of Designing Social Media Strategies

Figure 3.2	Process of designing social media strategies

Set Social Media Marketing Goals and Objectives	<ul><li>Analyze why the business should use social media marketing</li><li>Define the goals and objectives behind each social media marketing activity</li></ul>
Define and Understand the Target Audience	<ul><li>Collect and analyze data about your target audience</li><li>Data may be related to their age, income, location, occupation, social media sites frequented, needs, wants, preferences and buying behaviour.</li></ul>

Create a Social Media Marketing Mission Statement	• Create a social media marketing mission statement that would help remind you about your purpose for using social media. • The mission statement helps you know what you should be doing on social media to build your presence and brand image.
Create a Social Media Content Schedule and Calendar	• Create a social media marketing calendar to schedule the frequency of post on various social media marketing sites.
Identify Metrics to Measure Effectiveness	• Identify the metrics for measuring the effectiveness of the company's social media marketing campaign.
Use Social Media Management tools	• Use social media management tools to help in automatically posting content as per decided schedule as well as in creating and designing content & monitoring platform-centric analytics.
Track, Analyze, Adjust and Optimize	• Track results, evaluate and re-evaluate each step, and analyze the results. • Optimize by making all necessary changes wherever there is scope for improvement

Step 1: Set Social Media Marketing Goals and Objectives

As discussed, any strategy cannot be set without first defining the objectives you want to accomplish. We have seen what Social media objectives are. Setting specific goals makes it easy for you to measure your progress and assess the effectiveness of your strategy. When your goals are well-defined, you're able to decide specific actions and steps that you need to take in order to meet your business's needs. Outlining your goals also helps you decide on the budget as you get a clearer picture of how much you need to spend on the activities needed to achieve those goals.

You can use the "SMART Goal Setting Framework." SMART is an acronym for:

- **Specific:** Your goal must not be vague or unclear. It must be specific so that everyone can understand what it means.

- **Measurable:** Your goal must be trackable and measurable.

- **Achievable:** Your goal must be realistic and attainable with the resources at your disposal.

- **Relevant:** The goal should be relevant to your business. It should be in line with the overall business objectives in the current marketing environment.

- **Time-bound:** It is important for the goal to have a due date. Making the goal time-bound ensures that there is no procrastination.

A few examples of major social media marketing goals can be:

- Increase brand awareness by increasing the frequency of advertisements on social media, so that consumers become aware about the brand and its features.

- Create or improve brand image by engaging more with users and replying promptly to their comments and feedback within 24 hours.

- Increase website traffic by providing the website link in the social media advertisement or post.

- Provide customer service by addressing grievances and queries within 24 hours and providing helpful assistance to users whenever required.

- Increase sales by 10% in the next quarter by offering sales promotion offers such as discounts through the social media marketing campaigns.

- Generate leads by tracking page followers and users who comment, like, or share your post.

- Convert leads into customers by targeting your social media advertising to them and encouraging them to follow your page so that they receive product updates and reminders.

- Engaging with target customers by replying to their comments, sending thank you messages for following or liking the page, prompting them to post brand stories and experiences, and replying to them.

- Gaining insights about competitors by visiting their social media page and viewing their social media activity on a weekly or fortnightly basis.

- Increase your number of followers or community by prompt calls to action such "follow us now", "like us now", "share your product experiences through a post" etc.

- Receive customer feedback by encouraging users to share their feedback and user experience.

Step 2: Define and Understand the Target Audience

If you understand your target audience, you can develop a community, connect with them more effectively, and monitor the results and effectiveness of your marketing efforts. Moreover, it also saves money as you don't need to target your advertisements toward every single customer. You can, instead, craft more customized, personalized ads for a selected target audience.

Your target audience consists of those people who are most likely to be interested in buying your products or services. For example, if you have a sporting goods business, your target audience could be identified as fitness enthusiasts, outdoor enthusiasts, sportspersons, or athletes. You could also define your target audience as men aged between 18-34, swimmers, etc. Or, if your business sells beauty products and cosmetics, your target audience can be defined as working women aged 18-45. It depends on various factors such as your product type, prices, availability, market size, quality, and marketing objectives.

Process of defining the target audience

1. **Monitor your current audience:**
   First, you need to identify who is following you on social media. You must find out who likes, comments, and shares your posts. They will form an important part of your target audience. Additionally, you can identify the demographic profiles of your existing followers, and use them to target other people belonging to similar demographic profiles or possessing similar traits. For example, imagine you are a service provider offering various skill development courses. If you have found that your existing followers are MBA students from major cities, you can target other MBA students from those as well as other cities.

2. **Observe Competitors:**
   If you are new to social media or don't have a substantial number of followers currently, you can look at what your competitors are doing and follow suit. Observing the kind of target audience and followers your closest competitors have can give you useful insights. You can then target the

audience having similar demographic profiles, on the same social media platforms. In fact, observing competitors may also help you know *what not to do*. For example, if your competitor has run a marketing campaign on Facebook that hasn't received many likes, shares, views, or results, you can avoid following their footsteps and change your strategy.

3. **Define the demographic profile:**
   Demographics of your target audience include their:

   a. Location

   b. Gender

   c. Age group

   d. Occupation

   e. Education

   f. Lifestyle

   g. Culture

   h. Income levels

   i. Family size

   j. Interests and aspirations

These factors can give you insights into the buying behavior of your target audience, their geographical regions, their likes, dislikes, needs, wants, buying habits, purchasing power, and the social media platforms where they are active. Accordingly, you can build a niche of selected customers. For instance, after researching your target audience, you may discover that for your fresh-juice business, your target audience is college students in the

San Francisco Bay area. Or, if you're selling premium toys or premium children's products, you may want to target parents of toddlers in the US belonging to the upper-income class (with annual incomes above $156000). Or if you're selling protein bars, you may want to target people in the age group of 25-44 who are fitness enthusiasts.

4. **Use the available metrics tools:**
    Once you have identified the characteristics mentioned above such as age, gender, etc. you get a general idea of who you need to target. Now, you need to start to find them online. Most social media platforms provide specific tools that you can use for targeting your products and services. For example, Facebook gives you the option of using its Audience Insights tool which gives you aggregated information about people connected to your page and other people on Facebook.

5. **Conduct market research:**
    You can also conduct market research using online or offline surveys to identify your target audience. These surveys can be sent to your customers, prospects, and social media users via email or links on the social media page, telephonically, or in person. This kind of research will help you identify and understand demographic behavior, likes, dislikes, social media habits, expectations, and needs of the target audience.

Once the target audience is defined, you can identify which social media platforms they frequent. You can use one of several studies on social media demographics easily available online to understand which social media platforms your target audience is on. You can design customized content for these specific social media platforms in order to reach your target audience and make your marketing campaign more effective.

Example of social media demographics and usage (as of 2023):

Table 3.1   **Social media demographics and usage**

	Facebook	Instagram	Twitter	LinkedIn	Pinterest	YouTube
Number of Monthly Active Users	2.963 billion	2 billion	237.8 million	930 million	40 million	2.1 billion
Largest Age Group (in years)	25-34 (29%)	18-24 (30.8%)	18-29 (42%)	30-39 (31%)	25-34 (28.5%)	15-35 (77%)
Gender	44% Female 56% Male	48.2% Female 51.8% Male	34.1% Female 61.29% Male	43% Female 57% Male	76.2% Female 17% Male 6.6% unspecified	51.4% Female 48.6% Male
Time Spent Per Day	30 minutes	30.1 minutes	34.8 minutes	63% users access it weekly. 22% users access it daily	14.2 minutes	45.6 minutes

Source: Brent Bernhart. "Social media demographics to inform your brand's strategy in 2023" Sprout Social. April 28, 2023. https://sproutsocial.com/insights/new-social-media-demographics/

You can use data such as given in the figure above to identify where your target audience is and target them more effectively. If you own a women's apparel brand, you may decide to market your brand on Pinterest, YouTube, and Instagram to reach as many women as possible. Or if you are looking to market watches for youngsters (below 25), you may run your marketing campaigns on Instagram, Twitter, and YouTube.

Step 3: Create a Social Media Marketing Mission Statement

A mission statement provides direction and keeps you focused on your goals. It also provides purpose to your brand's online presence. In simple words, a social media mission statement is a formal declaration that summarizes your reasons, goals, and hopeful outcomes for having a social media presence.[56] Your mission statement must define what the social media presence will do for your brand and what you will do for your target audience. A mission statement must be clear and concise so that it will be easy for the audience to understand and remember. Some examples of mission statements are:

1. Our mission is to provide our clients with easier access to our products through Facebook and Instagram and enable them to connect, communicate, order, give feedback, and get excellent service.

2. We want to use LinkedIn to share our organizational culture with potential employees and guide them through our recruitment process to help them join our organization.

3. We want to use YouTube to share our product demos, tutorials, and reviews to guide users about product usage.

56. "Social Media Mission Statements: What Are They & How Do They Help Your Social Strategy? | Tallwave," Tallwave, June 6, 2022, https://tallwave.com/blog/social-media-mission-statements-what-are-they-how-do-they-help-your-social-strategy/#:~:text=Your%20social%20mission%20statement%20should,Comment%3F.

Step 4: Create a Social Media Content Schedule and Calendar

Social media content schedule

You must create a schedule for posting your content on social media. This schedule will describe when you will publish your content using a social media calendar. This schedule will help you identify where the content is overlapping, which social media sites are being utilized to what extent, and how often content is being posted. Additionally, it facilitates the coordination of content posting by a number of employees working for your company or for an outside party, like social media marketing companies. You can decide the frequency of posts per social media site per day, week, fortnight, or month as well as the timing of the post.

Specimen social media calendar

As seen above, a social media calendar is a good tool for planning your social media content scheduling. Let's take a look at a sample social media calendar. Suppose you have decided on the following content posting schedule:

- 1 post on Facebook daily at 9 a.m.

- 2 tweets on Twitter daily at 9 a.m. and 4 p.m. respectively.

- 1 Instagram reel/image/video a week every Friday evening at 6.

- 1 YouTube video each on the first and 3rd Saturday of every month, at 9 a.m.

Then, your social media calendar would look something like this (refer Figure 3.3)::

| Figure 3.3 | A social media calendar sample |

JANUARY, 2024

MONDAY	TUESDAY	WEDNESDAY	THURSDAY	FRIDAY	SATURDAY
					9 AM: 1 POST ON Facebook + 1 YouTube video + 1 weet 4 pm: 1 tweet
					1
9 AM: 1 POST ON Facebook + 1 Tweet 4 pm: 1 tweet	9 AM: 1 POST ON Facebook + 1 Tweet 4 pm: 1 tweet	9 AM: 1 POST ON Facebook + 1 Tweet 4 pm: 1 tweet	9 AM: 1 POST ON Facebook + 1 Tweet 4 pm: 1 tweet	9 AM: 1 POST ON Facebook + 1 Tweet 4 pm: 1 tweet 6 pm: 1 Instagram Reel	9 AM: 1 POST ON Facebook + 1 Tweet 4 pm: 1 tweet
2	**3**	**4**	**5**	**6**	**7**
9 AM: 1 POST ON Facebook + 1 Tweet 4 pm: 1 tweet	9 AM: 1 POST ON Facebook + 1 Tweet 4 pm: 1 tweet	9 AM: 1 POST ON Facebook + 1 Tweet 4 pm: 1 tweet	9 AM: 1 POST ON Facebook + 1 Tweet 4 pm: 1 tweet	9 AM: 1 POST ON Facebook + 1 Tweet 4 pm: 1 tweet 6 pm: 1 Instagram Reel	9 AM: 1 POST ON Facebook + 1 YouTube video + 1 Tweet 4 pm: 1 tweet
8	**9**	**10**	**11**	**12**	**13**

MONDAY	TUESDAY	WEDNESDAY	THURSDAY	FRIDAY	SATURDAY
9 AM: 1 POST ON Facebook + 1 Tweet 4 pm: 1 tweet	9 AM: 1 POST ON Facebook + 1 Tweet 4 pm: 1 tweet	9 AM: 1 POST ON Facebook + 1 Tweet 4 pm: 1 tweet	9 AM: 1 POST ON Facebook + 1 Tweet 4 pm: 1 tweet	9 AM: 1 POST ON Facebook + 1 Tweet 4 pm: 1 tweet 6 pm: 1 Instagram Reel	9 AM: 1 POST ON Facebook + 1 Tweet 4 pm: 1 tweet
14	15	16	17	18	19
9 AM: 1 POST ON Facebook + 1 Tweet 4 pm: 1 tweet	9 AM: 1 POST ON Facebook + 1 Tweet 4 pm: 1 tweet	9 AM: 1 POST ON Facebook + 1 Tweet 4 pm: 1 tweet	9 AM: 1 POST ON Facebook + 1 Tweet 4 pm: 1 tweet	9 AM: 1 POST ON Facebook + 1 Tweet 4 pm: 1 tweet 6 pm: 1 Instagram Reel	9 AM: 1 POST ON Facebook + 1 Tweet 4 pm: 1 tweet
20	21	22	23	24	25
9 AM: 1 POST ON Facebook + 1 Tweet 4 pm: 1 tweet	9 AM: 1 POST ON Facebook + 1 Tweet 4 pm: 1 tweet	9 AM: 1 POST ON Facebook + 1 Tweet 4 pm: 1 tweet	9 AM: 1 POST ON Facebook + 1 Tweet tweet	9 AM: 1 POST ON Facebook + 1 Tweet 4 pm: 1 tweet 6 pm: 1 Instagram Reel	9 AM: 1 POST ON Facebook + 1 Tweet 4 pm: 1 tweet
26	27	28	29	30	31

Step 5: Identify Metrics to Measure Effectiveness

Once you have fixed a schedule for your social media content, you will need to evaluate the effectiveness of your social media marketing campaign. You need to keep track of how well you're doing, whether there are any lacunae that need your attention, and whether there is any scope for improvement. Understanding the effectiveness of your social media marketing efforts helps you make optimum use of your resources and ensure that your efforts are not being wasted. Social media platforms are very dynamic and there are continuous updates and changes in algorithms, thus making it important to regularly monitor your social media marketing strategy using various metrics so that you can plan your next move. (Refer to Chapter 7 for detailed information on this topic)

Step 6: Use Social Media Management Tools

Marketing on social media is a tedious and time-consuming job. You need to continuously share posts, reply to comments, monitor your as well as your competitors' pages, and a lot more. Thankfully, there are some social media management tools that make this job much easier. They help manage your organic as well as targeted (paid) ads. Many of these tools are available online for free, and many also offer advanced paid options. Depending on your need and budget, you can select from one to many of these tools. Artificial Intelligence (AI) is of great help here. AI-based tools make your life easier and help you stay organized and they also allow you to get more things done in less time.

Here are some popular social media management tools that you can use:

Buffer: post scheduling, engagement, analytics, etc.

eClincher: post scheduling, monitoring keywords and hashtags, analytics, media library for images, auto-post, etc.

Hootsuite: managing and monitoring social media ads across 35 social media platforms, curating and scheduling content, measuring metrics, monitoring your social media presence, etc.

HubSpot: integrating all your marketing efforts into one platform, measuring your Return on Investment, understanding audience behavior such as when they are most active, the right time to post, etc.

Post Planner: content creation, post scheduling, monitoring your inboxes, etc.

MeetEdgar: content creation and scheduling, repurposing old content, analyzing content, etc.,

Sendible: creating customizable dashboards, content creation, preparing presentation-ready reports, etc. Designed for social media agencies having multiple clients.

Sprout Social: integrating all your marketing efforts into one platform, social media monitoring and analytics, and customer relationship management (CRM).

Social Bee: recycling evergreen content, sharing content across various social media sites from one place, analytics, etc.

Zoho Social: content scheduling, monitoring, social media analytics, and team collaboration

Social media management tools help you by offering the following functions:

Table 3.2 **Major functions of social media management tools**

Major Functions of Social Media Management tools		
Creating, customizing, and optimizing posts	Scheduling and publishing posts.	Cross-channel posting
Finding new fans or connecting with your existing ones.	Getting reports on various parameters such as followers, ROI, reach, engagement, website traffic, social share of voice, etc.	Performance tracking for finding out each post's effectiveness.
Content calendar overview	Competitor benchmarking	Generating and editing photos
Generating hashtags	In-depth analytics	Handling customer queries and reviews
Instantly responding to the audience	Influencer tracking	Measuring content performance
Managing multiple social media profiles across various platforms using a single dashboard	Creating or offering pre-made templates for creating content	Monitoring online conversations related to your brand.

Step 7: Track, Analyze, Adjust, and Optimize

In the fifth step (Refer: Point 3.2.5), you will identify various metrics for tracking the effectiveness of your social media marketing campaign. The final step in the social media marketing process is to use these metrics for continuously evaluating your marketing efforts. Tracking your social media marketing campaigns in real-time using various metrics will help you make the necessary tweaks wherever needed, instead of major, time-consuming changes. When you monitor and collect data, you gain insights into your target audience, helping you understand them better, which will in turn help you engage them more effectively. When you track your social media marketing campaign, you can also identify which content is performing well and which isn't. You can then focus on spotting the inadequacies in the low-performing content and rectifying those to adjust them to optimize your social media strategy. Identifying and analyzing your top-performing content will help you frame your future strategies.

Social media optimization is the process of improving your social posts (or your whole social media strategy) to achieve better results: faster follower growth, higher levels of engagement, more clicks or conversions, etc.[57] You can focus on key areas such as engagement, reach, growth in number of followers, conversions and overall performance to optimize your social media strategy. This step is crucial for your business as it will allow you to determine accountability as well as ensure that there is continuous growth in your numbers. Using social media management tools (discussed in the previous section) will help you with tracking, analyzing, adjusting, and optimizing the process.

---

57. Shannon Tien, "13 Easy Ways To Tackle Social Media Optimization," Social Media Marketing & Management Dashboard, July 19, 2023, https://blog.hootsuite.com/social-media-optimization/.

Quiz

1. _____ lays the base for control so that a company can manage any contingencies and check whether things are going as planned or if there are any changes required.

    a. Planning

    b. Strategy

    c. Metrics

    d. Media mix

2. With the help of a social media marketing plan, a company can determine its target audience, which social networks to join, as well as the type of content it needs to develop and share with its target audience.

    a. True

    b. False

3. Goals and objectives are the same.

    a. True

    b. False

4. **Identifying the target audience is important only for large enterprises. Smaller businesses don't need to perform this task..**

   a. True

   b. False

5. **The choice of social media marketing channels is important because–**

   a. Different social media platforms have audiences with different demographics.

   b. Companies can then design advertisements and content accordingly.

   c. Both a & b

   d. Neither a nor b

6. **_____help(s) in understanding the impact and effectiveness of the social media marketing plan on a company's revenues and marketing efforts.**

   a. Social media plans

   b. Social media strategies

   c. Metrics

   d. Social media marketing budget

7. A _____ shows what percentage of the marketing budget will be devoted to social media.

    a. social media marketing budget

    b. social media expense statement

    c. social media mix

    d. None of the above

8. Most companies spend between $200 and $350 per day i.e., between $6000 and $10500 a month on social media marketing.

    a. True

    b. False

9. According to Statista, companies in the US allocate about _____ % of their marketing budgets, on average, to social media marketing.

    a. 17

    b. 23

    c. 29

    d. 33

10. _____helps the company gain a better understanding and clarity about the market, customers, consumer behavior and demographics, seasonality, social media sites, their demographics, social media marketing trends, target audience, their behavior and preferences, etc.

a. Social media planning

b. Social media metrics

c. Marketing control

d. Market research

Answers	1 − a	2 − a	3 − b	4 − b	5 − c
	6 − c	7 − a	8 − a	9 − a	10 − d

Chapter Summary

◆ A social media marketing plan is a part or an extension of a company's marketing plan.

◆ Social media marketing planning is the structured process of researching and analyzing social media marketing situations, developing and documenting social media marketing objectives, strategies, and programs, and implementing, evaluating, and controlling social media marketing activities to achieve social media marketing goals.

◆ A social media marketing plan include the following: goals and objectives, target audience, social media channels, social media metrics, social media marketing budget, market research and content mix, and posting schedule.

◆ The process of social media marketing consists of the following steps:

   ▪ Setting social media marketing goals and objectives

   ▪ Defining and understanding the target audience

   ▪ Creating a social media marketing mission statement

   ▪ Creating a social media content schedule and calendar

   ▪ Identifying metrics to measure effectiveness

   ▪ Using social media management tools

   ▪ Tracking, analyzing, adjusting, and optimizing

◆ A plan is a statement of purpose regarding what action needs to be taken to achieve a goal or objective. A strategy, on the other hand, outlines how best to achieve that plan.

◆ A social media marketing strategy summarizes everything that a business plans to do, i.e., all the actions it plans to take to achieve its objectives on social media.

◆ A social media marketing strategy is a key ingredient of the social media marketing of a company.

◆ A few social media marketing strategies that businesses can adopt include analyzing the social media marketing scenario, setting clear and measurable goals, identifying and understanding the target audience, and creating a personal experience for them.

◆ Some more strategies include creating and nurturing a community; selecting and using the right metrics; deciding the best social media channels to use; using trendy, engaging, relevant, visually appealing, and attractive content; creating a social media calendar, keeping track of what competitors are doing; and adopting influencer marketing.

This page is intentionally left blank

Chapter 4

Content Designing for Social Media Platforms

As the previous chapters have established how important social media marketing is for any business, you need to be very careful with the kind of content you are sharing with your audience. Sharing the right type of content, at the right time, in the right manner, and with the right frequency is something that you need to master if you want your social media marketing strategy to succeed. This chapter elaborates on the basics of content creation and its process and discusses the content mix and various tools of content creation.

The key learning objectives should include the reader's understanding of the following:

- What is content creation and what are its basics?

- How do we create content for social media marketing?

- How do we identify the target audience and social media platforms to be used for marketing?

- What does the content mix contain?

- Which tools can one use for content creation?

- What are blogs, vlogs, and podcasts?

- What are infographics?

4.1 Content Creation

Social media content includes written content, videos, photographs, audio, live streams, graphics, etc. created for various social media platforms. The process of creating these is known as content creation. One of the most challenging and interesting tasks in social media marketing is creating content.

Content creation is the process where you generate ideas and create written or visual content for communicating those ideas to your intended buyers. Good content helps in increasing brand loyalty and reach. Content can take many forms. These include blogs, vlogs, posts, videos, tweets, graphics, eBooks, advertisements, and much more. Even though content has so many forms, content creation isn't as simple as it may seem, and is pretty nuanced. Studies have shown that good content induces customers to buy products, which means that the likelihood of their purchases increases significantly. Jalal R. Hanaysha[58] (2022)

---

58. Jalal Rajeh Hanaysha, "Impact of Social Media Marketing Features on Consumer's Purchase Decision in the Fast-Food Industry: Brand Trust as a Mediator," International Journal of Information Management Data Insights 2, no. 2 (November 1, 2022): 100102, https://doi.org/10.1016/j.jjimei.2022.100102.

found that various dimensions of social media marketing such as interaction, perceived relevance, and informativeness are found as significant predictors of purchase decisions. The quality of information available to consumers "pulled" them towards the brand, i.e., it created consumer demand for the brand. Nur Syakirah Ahmada et al.[59] (2015) say that companies need to focus more on social media content marketing to attract more consumers to engage with their brands.

Content helps generate leads, earn revenue, and build a strong customer base. too. It also helps in attracting new visitors to the company's web or social media page, thus increasing traffic. You can also evaluate the content that had the most success on a given social media platform by seeing the number of comments, what the comments say, as well as the traffic (in terms of views, likes, and clicks) and shares on the platform. Since social media has a huge reach, it can be a brilliant platform for increasing brand recognition, brand image, and loyalty.

4.2 Process of Content Creation

When you creating content for your business, you must ensure that you are creating and sharing content that will be most effective in achieving your marketing goals. The content must *educate and entertain* the audience for it to have a greater impact on them. For this, you must understand the process of content creation, the four C's of content creation, and the major types of content. Once you understand the major types of content, you can select the ones most suitable for achieving your

---

59. Nur Syakirah Ahmad, Rosidah Musa, and Mior Harris Mior Harun, "The Impact of Social Media Content Marketing (SMCM) towards Brand Health," Procedia. Economics and Finance 37 (January 1, 2016): 331–36, https://doi.org/10.1016/s2212-5671(16)30133-2.

marketing objectives. Additionally, you must know how to design the content mix and use the varieties of content creation tools available at your disposal.

The basic process of content creation is as follows:

Figure 4.1 **Content creation process**

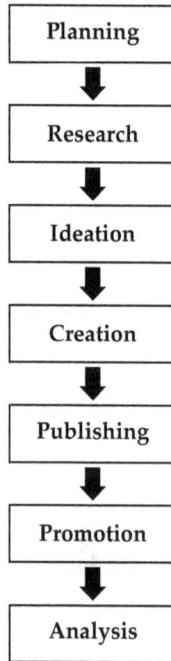

```
┌──────────────┐
│   Planning   │
└──────────────┘
       ↓
┌──────────────┐
│   Research   │
└──────────────┘
       ↓
┌──────────────┐
│   Ideation   │
└──────────────┘
       ↓
┌──────────────┐
│   Creation   │
└──────────────┘
       ↓
┌──────────────┐
│  Publishing  │
└──────────────┘
       ↓
┌──────────────┐
│  Promotion   │
└──────────────┘
       ↓
┌──────────────┐
│   Analysis   │
└──────────────┘
```

1. Planning:

You must first plan the process of content creation. This includes deciding the objectives of the content, the target audience, i.e., whom the content is intended for, what type of content is needed or suitable for achieving the objectives, and the competitors' content.

2. Research:

The content creation process is incomplete without research. You need to find out what kind of content resonates with your audience, what your audience likes and dislikes, what they expect, and what they are interested in. This research also includes finding out what the latest buzzwords, trends, topics of conversation. and the top keywords. Moreover, researching what other competitors in the market is essential too.

3. Ideation:

Once the planning and research are done and the keywords are identified, you need content ideas. These ideas include what should be the topic of the content, its theme, and what form it will be in (a blog or a vlog, a post on a social media page, a podcast, a video, or an image). Once the ideas are in place, they should be evaluated and the best ones, i.e., the ones most suitable to achieve your objectives should be selected.

4. Creation:

Though content creation may include creating videos, graphics, images, and audio, writing remains a fundamental part of it. You need to write a message to the audience through a caption or description, explaining the theme (such as Black History Month, Valentine's Day), purpose (Demonstration of how to use), or expected outcome (Learn to make pasta at home) of the content.

Imagine introducing a new mobile phone. You'd create a video showcasing the unboxing, turning on the phone, displaying its look, and sharing sample pictures and videos. To help potential buyers, you'd also need written content, like ratings (e.g., 4/5 for the camera, 3/5 for video quality) and comparisons with other phones on the market. This mix of visuals and details aims to assist customers in making informed purchase decisions.

5. Publishing:

Once the content has been created, it may need to be edited if required. Editing can be done immediately or as an ongoing process. The finalized content is then uploaded to the decided social media platforms and published. Many content creators use content management software for publishing. With the help of this software, you can decide on a schedule through which posts can be uploaded regularly -- once a week on a specific day of the week, fortnightly, and so on. You can immediately publish or select a specific date and time in the future to publish the selected content. This kind of scheduling makes your job slightly easier. (Refer to the specimen social media calendar in Chapter 3)

6. Promotion:

After the content is published, you must promote it so that it reaches the maximum number of people. You can use various social media platforms, websites, and pay-per-click advertisements to promote your content. This can be done by identifying which medium is used more by the targeted audience and then selecting that medium to promote the content. For example: In the above example, a video explaining the features of a mobile phone was created. Suppose it was published on YouTube. You can promote this video on your Facebook Page, Instagram, or as a pay-per-click advertisement on social media pages which will redirect the customer to the video.

7. Analysis:

The final step in the process of content creation is to analyze the published content. You must gauge the responses to the posted content in the form of traffic, likes, responses, page views, shares, subscriptions, etc.

Basically, the analysis includes evaluating the following parameters:

- **Page views:** How many users have visited and viewed the particular piece of content.

- **Engagement rates:** This includes the number of users who engage with the content through likes, comments, shares, etc.

- **Audience growth:** This includes the number of new users or prospects who subscribe to the page after viewing the content.

- **Bounce rate:** This is the number of people who visit the page but leave only after viewing the content and do not further engage or visit more pages. This helps in identifying how many users do not like the content or are dissatisfied with it.

- **Conversion rate:** This shows how many users get converted into customers by either filling out some form or purchasing the product.

- **Time on page:** This shows how much time users spend on the page reading the content. Do they consume the entire content or do they leave midway? Do they watch/read the content more than once and dedicate more time to it?

- **Paid and organic traffic:** Organic traffic is made up of the users who visit the site through unpaid sources like search engines that aren't paid for. Paid traffic, on the other hand, is traffic generated from paid sources like social media advertisements, sponsored search engine ads, etc.

4.3 The Four Cs of Content Marketing

Figure. 4.2 **Four Cs of content creation**

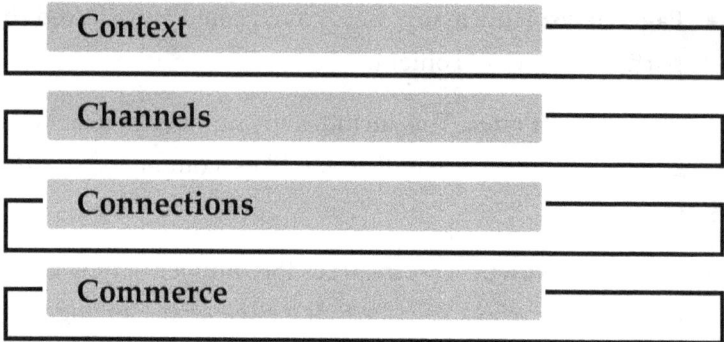

Context
Channels
Connections
Commerce

1. Context

Context is the theme of the content and the message that you want to communicate to the audience. The context should not only be relevant but also appealing enough to interest and attract the audience. Marketers must decide the context of the content carefully, as it will not be effective if the target audience finds it irrelevant or uninteresting.

2. Channel

A channel is the medium selected for the content, i.e. the vehicle that would carry your message. For example, a blog may be shared on a social media page, a website, or via e-mail. There are a multitude of channels available for you to select based on the type of message you want to send across and the type of audience you want to reach. Channel selection is an important decision as the choice of the channel is directly related to the types of users using that particular channel and whether they constitute your target audience. Moreover, the form of the content also changes with changes in channels. For example, a long video on YouTube may be converted into a reel on Instagram or a long post with images on Facebook.

3. Connections

Connections include prospects, customers, users, and the target market. One of the main goals of content is to engage the audience and build relationships with them over time. Hence, you must design content that will keep the audience engaged and ensure that they like and share the content, thus increasing its reach. Marketers should conduct in-depth research into who constitutes their target audience and what makes them click. Knowing what are the likes, dislikes, areas of interest, buying habits, preferences, expectations, needs, and wants of the connections will help marketers design relevant content that would be more effective.

4. Commerce

A major goal of content is also to generate business and earn revenue. Content that engages customers and creates a good brand image will entice customers to purchase the product/ service. Content helps answer the queries of customers, provides them with relevant information, and assists them with the buying process. Content may lead the customer to buy in-app or redirect them to the website to generate sales. There is no point if marketers have great content that isn't translating into revenue, customer engagement, and brand image. Therefore, marketers should work towards making the content more engaging, attractive, appealing, and persuasive.

4.4 Major Forms of Content

Let us look at some of the most common and major forms of content:

Types of content

Major Forms of Content

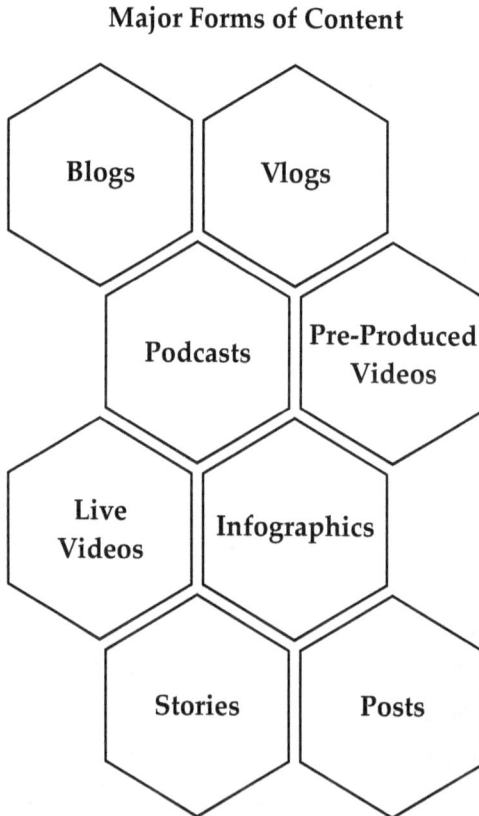

1. Blogs

A "blog" is "a regularly updated website or web page, typically one run by an individual or small group, which is written in an informal or conversational style."[60]

A blog is an important part of the content mix because it can drive traffic to your website and give you a platform to provide value to your customers. According to The State of Content Marketing Report 2023 by Semrush, blogs are one of the most effective ways to connect with the target audience.[61]

Blogs help in setting the SEO (Search Engine Optimization) marketing strategy. In simple words, SEO is the process of improving your website's visibility on search engines such as Google, Bing, etc. It helps to increase the quality as well as quantity of the organic traffic coming to your webpage. Blogs also help in improving your business' search results on SERPs (Search Engine Result Page). SERP is the list of results that are shown when a user enters a search query. There are 2 kinds of results here: organic ones that are generated by the search engine's algorithms and paid ones that are generated from advertisements. The results are displayed in descending order based on relevance. If you maintain an up-to-date blog by regularly sharing fresh content encompassing topics that people are interested in, it helps the blog become more effective. Well-written blogs help you establish yourself as an authority in the field. For example, there are many well-established makeup blogs that users refer to before purchasing cosmetics. These blog posts will also contain prominent keywords of your industry, helping your post rank well in SERPs.

60. Olivia Atkinson, "What Is Blogging And Why Is It Important For Building Material Businesses?," Insynth (blog), March 15, 2023, https://www.insynth.co.uk/blog/what-is-a-blogging-and-why-is-it-important-for-building-material-businesses.

61. Zach Paruch, "12 Types of Content Marketing to Leverage for Success in 2023," Semrush Blog, May 3, 2023, https://www.semrush.com/blog/types-of-content-marketing/.

Makeup and Beauty Blog features daily product reviews, makeup tips, and beauty news. In the 10 years since its beginning, it has amassed over 101 million page views, 11,500 posts, and visits from 227 countries. It covers more than 120 different makeup and beauty brands and is run by freelancer and makeup and beauty expert Karen Monterichard.

Source: https://makeupandbeautyblog.com/about/

A few ideas for you to blog about are:

1. Take a current topic or event and link it to your marketing. For example: A toyshop could blog about "Best gifts for kids this Christmas." The list of gifts could include toys from this shop as well as a link to their product page.

2. Identify the trends going on in your industry and write about them and relate them to your product. For example, during the Covid-19 pandemic, the Dalgona coffee trend became very popular. A coffee manufacturer, say Nestle, can write about this trend and explain how Dalgona coffee tastes better when made with Nescafe instant coffee powder.

3. You can ask popular or top industry experts to weigh in on a topic and then compile their views into a blog. For example, an educational institute could write a blog with insights from top recruiters about "How to crack job

Interviews" and they can then relate it to courses offered by the educational institute that teach students these skills.

4. Search for recent questions and doubts that customers have posted about your product or service online and write a blog addressing all these doubts. For example, a personal care products manufacturer finds many questions about skincare for acne such as which moisturizer, toner, or creams to use. The manufacturer could address these questions through a blog about common skincare questions for acne-ridden skin and market their products.

2. Vlogs

A video blog, also known as a video log or vlog is a type of blog in which the majority of the content is in the form of videos. Vlogs contain embedded video with supporting images, text, and other metadata. Vlogs can be posted in one take or regularly updated.

For example, some technology vlogs demonstrate how to use certain appliances, gadgets, operating systems, or software. Makeup vlogs have makeup tutorial videos or review videos of products like lipsticks, foundation, mascaras, etc. Travel vlogs feature videos of beautiful locations, things to do , spots to visit, places to stay and dine at, etc.

Vlogging is a very useful tool for marketers to inform and educate their customers about their products or services. Vlogs are popular because customers get a sense of transparency and personal communication while watching the videos.

Launched in October 2015 as a YouTube Channel, Technical Guruji is a vlog by Gaurav Chaudhary. Gaurav posts videos related to technology in the Hindi language. What struck a chord with audiences was that he didn't just post product reviews but explained various concepts and how technology worked. Catering to over 15 million subscribers, Technical Guruji is the largest tech YouTube channel in India. His vlogging channel is also the largest vlog in India with over three million subscribers. [62]

3. Podcasts

Podcasts are a type of digital media, usually audio, that are available in a series of episodes or parts and are streamed or downloaded by an end user over the Internet.[63]

A podcast series contains discussions about particular topics by one or multiple hosts. They provide additional links, notes, information, commentary, and forums (for discussion by the audience of the podcast). Podcasters record and upload podcasts on channels like YouTube, Spotify, Instagram, X, Facebook, etc which can then be "streamed" or listened to.

There are over 2.8 million podcasts in the world. Podcasts are important to businesses as they can share their knowledge and expertise with customers, giving a one-to-one communication experience. Customers can also give their feedback and address

62. Pranit Sarda, "Gaurav Chaudhary: Your 'Technical Guruji'," Forbes India, February 12, 2020, https://www.forbesindia.com/article/30-under-30-2020/gaurav-chaudhary-your-039technical-guruji039/57639/1.

63. All Posts by Margaret Rouse, "What Is a Podcast? - Definition from Techopedia," Techopedia, October 16, 2023, https://www.techopedia.com/definition/5546/podcast.

their queries to the podcasters, making it an engaging tool.

> The American Life is an American weekly radio show that also has a weekly podcast that is downloaded by more than 2.5 million people. It is hosted by Ira Glass and has won most of the major broadcasting awards. It contains interesting, thought-provoking, and heart-warming stories over hour-long episodes shared each week. It is the best example of how one can crossover from a traditional medium like radio to a digital medium successfully.

4. Pre-produced videos

Pre-produced videos are short-form videos that are created specially for social media to increase engagement and grab the attention of viewers on social media.

Pre-produced videos are not streamed live but recorded by the marketer/influencer beforehand, edited, and then posted at a specific time. They may be advertisement videos, interviews with Q&A sessions, product videos, promotional offers, contests, announcements, product launches, etc.

Videos are interesting to watch and give out marketing messages in an entertaining mannerInstagram allows users to create and share videos of different kinds. Users can upload short videos (of up to 90 seconds) known as reels and longer videos (up to 60 minutes) as well. If you have a public account, posting reels under 90 seconds helps to become eligible for recommendations and get more reach. These reels help users share creative and entertaining content, market products and brands, or just have fun. Instagram also allows you to post Instagram stories with videos of up to 60 seconds. Some social media platforms have videos of less than 10 seconds which are short yet informative.

> ### Some popular video ads on Facebook:
>
> - Kleenex's Ultra Soft Ad
> - Apple's Ad with Taylor Swift: #Taylor Vs. Treadmill
> - Low Battery Anxiety by LG

5. Live videos

Another popular form of content is live videos. According to Corporate Communications,[64] live videos have a 148% higher organic reach than any other form of content. Live streaming a video turns it from a broadcast into a conversation, thus making it more appealing to the audience. It has a high level of engagement due to its very nature. Live videos help in getting instant feedback along with creating a connection with the audience. Most of the major social media platforms including Facebook have prioritized live content in their algorithms, thus making it an appealing tool for marketers. In fact, Facebook claims that live videos get more than six times the interactions than pre-recorded videos.

---

64. "The Benefits of Live Video on Social Media," Corporate Communications, Inc., n.d., https://www.corporatecomm.com/blog/the-benefits-of-live-video-on-social-media.

Fun Facts:

- Facebook Live videos get over 10 times more comments than pre-produced videos.

- Facebook Live videos produce six times as many interactions as traditional videos.

- 45% of US Livestream viewers between the ages of 18-34 watch live stream content on Instagram, followed by YouTube with 31%.[65]

6. Infographics

An infographic is a visual representation of any type of data or information. Infographics include many different elements, such as text, images, graphs, charts, icons, emojis, and/or diagrams to convey messages. Infographics help present information quickly and efficiently. Businesses use infographics because customers get access to information at a glance which, due to its pictorial form, is easy to understand, attractive, and interesting.

For example, a mobile phone company can create an infographic of a newly launched mobile phone mentioning its specifications, key features, and benefits.

Following is an example of a Starbucks infographic titled "Every bag of coffee tells a story. Thank you for supporting our farmers and their communities."

---

65. Growthoid. "Instagram Live Statistics [Data for 2023]." July 7, 2023. https://growthoid.com/instagram-live-statistics/

| Figure 4.4 | **A Starbucks infographic** |

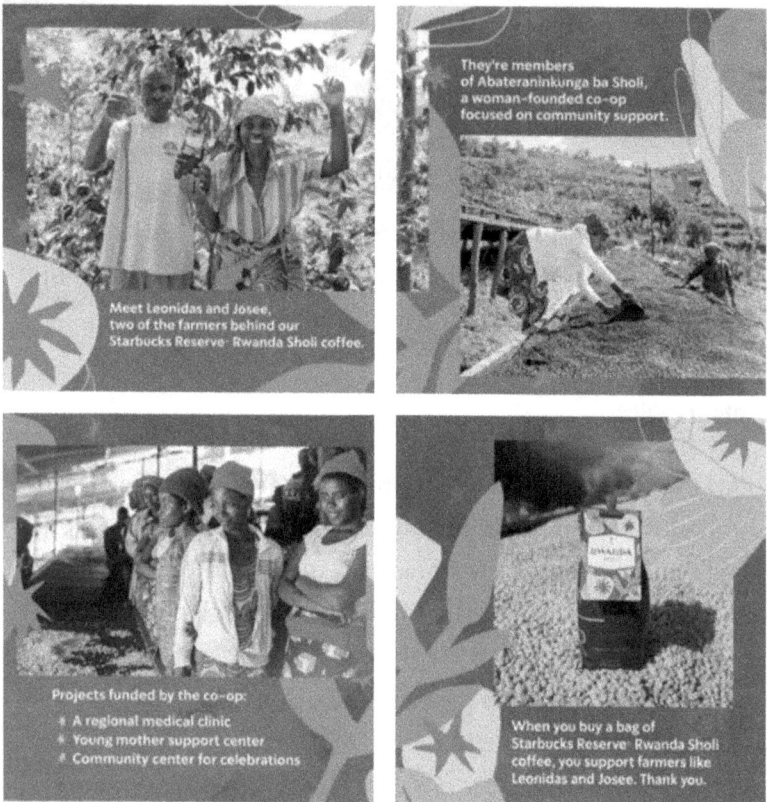

Source: https://m.facebook.com/story.php?story_fbid=10161288640278057&id
=22092443056&mibextid=CDWPTG

7. Posts

A social media post is a type of content or message that
is published on any social media platform such as Facebook,
Instagram, Twitter, LinkedIn, etc. A post can take various forms—
text, images, videos, audio, and webpage links. Posts are beneficial
in explaining something in detail and also allow you to caption
your images and videos. Posts are suitable for sharing evergreen,
high-value content designed to reach a larger audience. They
appear in the users' feed and since most users scroll with the

sound turned off, they are suitable for soundless content. Posts are permanent in nature and stay on your social media page forever unless you delete them.

8. Stories

A new form of posts is Stories, made popular by Instagram and Facebook. While posts are permanent, stories are short-term and have a lifespan of just 24 hours. After 24 hours they are automatically deleted. Users can share text, images, videos, or a combination of these in their stories. Business users on Instagram having over 100,00 followers get access to an additional feature of stories, viz. the "swipe-up" feature. Using this feature, you can get click-throughs to your website directly from an Instagram story. Stories are suitable for you if you're looking to share fresh, current, short-term content, which is more casual. Instagram stories are best used for sharing breaking news, conducting polls, sharing casual selfies, behind-the-scenes videos, and short-term sales promotion offers such as discounts and contests.

4.5 Designing the Content Mix

Till this point, we have seen what is meant by content and the process of content creation. Now let us take a look at what is a content mix, and how it helps a business market its products on social media.

Content marketing mix is "the right blend of different content types (blogs, videos, case studies, webinars, podcasts, e-books, infographics, and so on) to attract, engage, convert, and retain your ideal customers."[66]   You need to find the perfect content mix that will create the best value for your customers as well as you. Before delving into the content mix strategy, let us see the various types of content.

For designing the content mix, you must first identify your audience. For example, you want to market a new digital marketing course for MBA students, which will help them learn new skills and get a certification, which will, in turn, help them get jobs. So your target audience is MBA students.

Next, you must define your marketing objectives. For example, if the course is new, your objective would be to conduct trials and have students enroll in the course by giving them information about it. So your marketing objectives would be to create awareness about the course you're offering, give them additional information about the course content, duration, pricing, and benefits, and persuade students to enroll for the course.

The next step would be selecting the content. You may decide to create a post giving basic information about the course. Interested students can then check out videos explaining the course content in detail. You may also decide to post sales promotion offers using an infographic highlighting offers such as a discount on enrolling within a certain period of time, or cashback for referring the course to others. So the content you finalize may include a simple informative post, a video, or an infographic containing the sales promotion offer.

Then comes the actual content creation. You may have an in-

---

66. Elise Dopson, "The Shift in Your Content Marketing Mix: 25 Marketers On What's Changed in 2 Years I Databox Blog," Databox, October 9, 2023, https://databox.com/perfect-content-marketing-mix#:~:text=Mix%20in%202021-,What%20is%20a%20Content%20Mix%3F,and%20retain%20your%20ideal%20customers.

house content team who may write the post content, design the infographic, and shoot the video. The content creators may use various online content creation tools that generate your desired content easily. Alternatively, you may hire a content creation agency or freelancers to do the job.

Once the content is ready, you need to publish it. For this, you should have identified social media platforms, groups, or communities where you can publish the content. Here, there are two kinds of marketing you can use. One is organic marketing where you post the content on your own social media pages such as your Facebook, Instagram, and YouTube pages, and provide links to your website. The other is paid marketing where you can publish your content in the form of an ad for which you will need to pay Facebook, Instagram, and YouTube to showcase your ads to the target audience.

Finally, you need to monitor your content, respond to customer queries and comments, and evaluate the content based on how many views, likes, and responses it has received and how many students have enrolled in your courses. You can also compare the different forms of content to find out which was more effective, and which channel got more responses or generated the most website traffic. This will help you in managing your future content more effectively.

4.6 Content Creation Tools

With the advances that technology has made, content creators have their work made easy with a bevy of digital tools available for content creation. There are thousands of such tools, some of which are available free of cost online, whereas others can be purchased or subscribed to. You can use these tools to make your job easier and more effective. Using these tools, you can create a huge variety of content such as text, images, videos, GIFs, infographics, and much more. By using the right content creation tools, you can accelerate the process, gain new and different insights, and produce more effective content.

Let us take a look at a few of the most popular ones used for content creation:

Figure 4.5	Popular content creation tools
Canva	• Canva is the most popular content creation tool. It is used for creating graphics for social media. • Canva enables users to create high-quality pictures quickly with the help of a range of social media templates, layouts and design elements. These can be customized to create unique designs. • Using Canva, one can create professional looking photographs as well as videos. • Companies can plan, create and publish their social media posts directly from Canva.

Crello	<ul><li>Crello is also a popular content creation tool which has many customizable templates, designs, and layouts along with millions of high quality photos and videos.</li><li>It is similar to Canva but while Canva is a great option for designing static graphics, Crello, on the other hand, is a better option for designing animated graphics.</li><li>What differentiates Crello from Canva is that Crello offers over 180 million photos, 15,000 illustrations, 30,000 free design templates and 32,000 videos.</li><li>It allows designing by a team of up to 10 members and also offers a music library. Crello too provides tools to design templates specifically for social media.</li></ul>
Promo	<ul><li>Promo was launched in 2016 to dispute the way in which videos were made.</li><li>They are Facebook and Instagram Marketing Partners and YouTube Videos Creative Partners.</li><li>Users can access ready-made video templates along with fully licensed high-quality music, attractive text which can be customized, and an award-winning editor.</li></ul>

Adobe Express	• Adobe Express has replaced Adobe Spart as a content creation tool for social media.
	• Adobe Express lets anyone create beautiful web stories, combining text and graphics. It allows users to easily create animated videos.
	• There is no filming required; users can just speak their story which can then be customized with theme, icons, images and text.
	• Adobe Express provides thousands of unique templates, design assets, Adobe Stock royalty-free photos, and more.
Anchor	• Anchor is one of the most popular platforms for creation, distribution and monetization of podcasts. It is free for all users.
	• It can be incorporated with all major podcasting outlets as well as free social media sites for audio.
	• It allows easy distribution with the help of Spotify – an audio disruptor. Using Anchor users can analyze podcast performance with analytics through engagement insights.
	• Using the anchor app, users can easily create and share videos, and audio recordings. It is especially popular among businesses and users looking to share their podcast on various social media platforms.

Infogram	• Infogram is a web-based platform for data visualization and infographics where users can make and share digital charts, infographics and maps based on the data they provide. • Infogram's editor helps convert data provided by users into infographics and reports that can be downloaded, published or shared • It offers ready-to-use templates, customized templates, animations and interactive charts and maps which make the content attractive, impressive and engaging.
Visme	• Visme is another popular social media marketing content creation tool. It can be used to create professional presentations, engaging videos, interesting infographics and beautiful designs along with other branded content. • Users can work in teams and collaborate, communication and move from draft to format quickly. • It offers a lot of options from simple visuals to completely interactive content.

Animaker	<ul><li>Animaker is a platform which can be used by beginners, non-designers as well as professionals for crating animated and live-action videos.</li><li>Animaker has been used by over 15 million people worldwide and many top brands like Bosch, Target, Standard Chartered, etc. to create their social media marketing content.</li><li>Users can create their own animated characters, and access over 100 million stock photos and images.</li><li>They can select from 1000+ templates, upload and edit 4k videos and get the content instantly resized for social media.</li></ul>

A few more content creation tools:

- Animoto
- Placeit
- CapCut
- Prezi
- Piktochart
- Copy.ai
- Lumen 5

- Stencil
- Fotor
- Snappa
- Fotojet
- Headliner
- Google Sheets
- Giphy Capture

Quiz

1. **Blogs, vlogs, posts, videos, tweets, graphics, eBooks, advertisements, etc. are types of–**

   a. Social media strategies

   b. Social media content

   c. Social media plans

   d. None of the above

2. **The following are the basics of content creation except–**

   a. Choosing the appropriate data for the target audience.

   b. Putting oneself in the audience's shoes in order to understand what content they expect, like, and dislike.

   c. Checking the competitors' content.

   d. Writing inconsistent content that confuse your target audience.

3. **A social media content creator for social media _____ text, audio, videos, images, and graphics.**

   a. only creates

   b. creates and publishes

   c. only publishes

   d. neither creates nor publishes

4. _____is the specific group of consumers most likely to want your product or service, and therefore, the group of people who should see your ad campaigns.

   a. Target audience

   b. Target users

   c. Target market

   d. Target customers

5. The _____ is a part of the _____that the advertisement or content is intended for.

   a. target market; target audience

   b. target audience; target market

   c. target customer; target market

   d. target user; target audience

6. Elaborate posts can be shared on _____which can contain text, images, videos, or graphics and users can comment, reply, like, and share the posts.

   a. Twitter

   b. YouTube

   c. Facebook

   d. All of the above

7. _____ is the first step in the content creation process.

   a. Research

   b. Strategy

   c. Planning

   d. Evaluating

8. The step in the content creation process that decides what should be the topic of the content and its theme, what form it will be in, whether it will a blog or a vlog, or a post on a social media page, a podcast, or a video or an image is called–

   a. Planning

   b. Research

   c. Analysis

   d. Ideation

9. Which of the following statements about content creation is not true?

   a. Editing content is a continuous process.

   b. Content can be scheduled daily or weekly.

   c. After the content is published, the content creator must promote it so that it reaches maximum people.

   d. Organic traffic is generated from paid sources.

10. What are the four Cs of content creation?

a. Communication, context, courtesy, collaboration

b. Context, channels, communications, commerce

c. Context, continuity, communications, commerce

d. Communication, courtesy, collaboration, commerce

Answers	1 – b	2 – d	3 – b	4 – a	5 – b
	6 – c	7 – c	8 – d	9 – d	10 – b

Chapter Summary

◆ Social media content includes written content, videos, photographs, and graphics created for various social media platforms. The process of creating these is known as content creation.

◆ One of the most time-consuming tasks in social media marketing is to create content.

◆ Content creates value, attracts customers, engages and retains them.

◆ Content creators must identify the right target audience and the right social media platform for the content to be effective.

◆ The content creation process includes the following steps: Planning, Research, Ideation, Creation, Publishing, Promotion, and Analysis.

◆ Context, channels, communications, and commerce are the four Cs of content creation.

◆ The major types of content include blogs, vlogs, podcasts, pre-produced videos, live videos, infographics, posts, and stories.

◆ There are thousands of tools for content creation that help content creators in designing and publishing quality content. Some of the popular ones include Canva, Crello, Flipsnack, Promo, Adobe Express, Anchor, Infogram, Visme and Animaker.

This page is intentionally left blank

Chapter **5**

Facebook, Instagram, and Threads Marketing

F acebook, Instagram, and Threads, all owned by Meta, have emerged as the strongest social media marketing platforms due to their popularity, features, and huge user bases. This chapter gives an overview of these platforms, their characteristics, the types of posts users can share using these platforms, and the organic and paid ways that you can use to market your brands/products on Facebook and Instagram.

The key learning objectives should include the reader's understanding of the following:

- How to use Facebook, Instagram, and Threads for marketing?

- How to use Facebook and Instagram for advertising?

- What are the characteristics of Facebook marketing?

- What are the characteristics of Instagram marketing?

- What are the various types of posts and their dimensions?

5.1 Facebook Marketing

Facebook marketing is the practice of promoting a brand and maintaining its presence on Facebook. It refers to both organic (free) postings/interactions, and paid, or "boosted" posts.[67]

Organic marketing is when users see your posts or messages without paid distribution. It may include posts on the news feeds seen by your page followers, shared/liked by users and seen by their friends, and your interactions with the users. Paid marketing, on the other hand, includes attracting users through paid advertising.

---

67. "Facebook Marketing for Ecommerce: What It Means and Best Practices," BigCommerce, n.d., https://www.bigcommerce.com/ecommerce-answers/what-is-facebook-marketing/.

Businesses market on Facebook in the following ways:

| Figure 5.1 | Types of Facebook marketing |

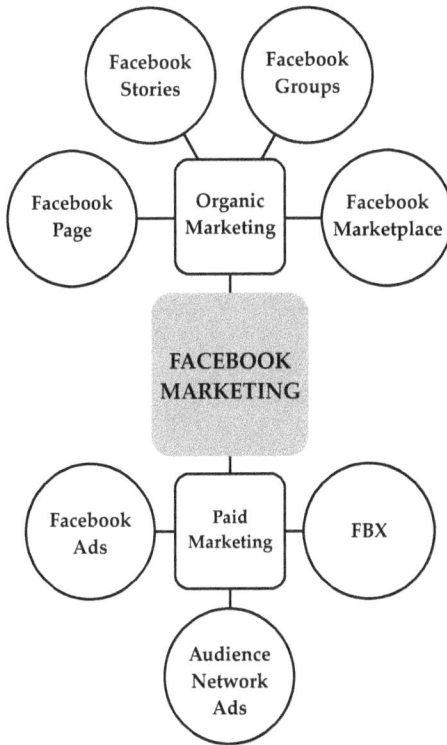

5.1.1 Organic Marketing on Facebook

1. Facebook page

Businesses/brands publish their Facebook pages where they can identify themselves. You do so by setting up the page, and posting content in the form of videos and images about your products and services. A Facebook page is a good way of communicating with customers, targeting new markets, reaching the target audience, and increasing brand awareness. Users may visit the page, like it, like and comment on the posts, and engage with the brand. Users who like the page can see more updates and receive notifications when new posts are posted on the page. This is an organic way of marketing your brand, hence you can use this even if you have budget constraints.

| Figure 5.2 | Starbucks' Facebook page explaining the benefits of a Starbucks card |

Source: https://www.pinterest.com/pin/the-art-of-the-facebook-page-design--104356916334960752/

2. Post types

When you share anything on Facebook using your timeline, it is called a post. You can post text, images, videos, and many more things to your timelines which you can share with other users in your network (your followers). Both general users as well as business users can post content to their timelines. Following are the kinds of posts that you can share on your Facebook page:

Text posts

You can share simple text on your posts which are also called status updates. These posts contain text only, without any images or videos. Text posts are useful while sharing quotes and simple questions that don't require polling or announcements. Text posts aren't the best choice when you aim to drive traffic to your website or increase your sales. However, they are a very good option for sharing information quickly, like details about an upcoming product launch, dates, and venues; sparking conversations with and among users and educating your followers. When you are looking to receive feedback from your users, a text post can be a good choice.

Photo posts

Posts that include a photo are likely to generate more engagement than an average post as they are visually appealing.. Hence, you must use photos whenever possible. Whether it's a product image, an attractive photo, or even user-generated content, photo posts are highly popular. Photo posts are especially useful to businesses looking to attract new customers.

It is said that a picture says a thousand words, and that is why photo posts are effective in conveying messages to the audience. With Facebook being cluttered with many advertisements, users, and businesses, it's important for you to stand out from the crowd. Photo posts are a great way to do this and they also help capture the attention of users.

Video posts

Videos are one of the most popular formats for Facebook posts. In fact, video posts have been shown to perform better than all other forms of content on Facebook. An average of 100 million hours of videos are watched daily by Facebook users globally.[68] You can use video posts to promote your products and create brand awareness.

What makes videos so popular is that they are incredibly engaging and they promote interaction. Moreover, videos play automatically on users' news feeds (can be toggled on/off by the user), making it important for you to make the first few seconds of your video as appealing as possible. You must, however, note that some users play videos without sound, hence while creating videos, you should optimize them to play without sound, with the help of captions. Facebook allows videos of any length to be uploaded and hence, video posts are a valuable tool for businesses.

Link posts

A link post is used to share an external link. This could be a link to your business website, to a blog, or an e-commerce site's product page.

For sharing a link post, you must copy and paste the URL into the Create Post box. Then, Facebook automatically generates a preview of the website that the link will take users to. Link posts are helpful in promoting your own website content or bringing

68. Social Shepherd Ltd, "33 Essential Facebook Statistics You Need To Know In 2023," The Social Shepherd, June 26, 2023, https://thesocialshepherd.com/blog/facebook-statistics#:~:text=An%20average%20of%20100%20million,video%20views%20are%20gained%20daily.

the attention of the audience to some other content that they might enjoy or benefit from, like a blog recommending your products, or a vlog specifying how to use them. Links are also effective in driving traffic to your e-commerce site.

Pinned posts

A pinned post is any Facebook post that is saved (pinned) to the top of your Facebook page. When a post is pinned, no matter how someone reaches your Facebook page, the pinned post will be the first post the users see.

Pinned posts are useful when there is critical information that needs to be shared or if you want to highlight a very well-performing post. You can also use pinned posts for sales promotion, introducing and creating awareness about new products, or sharing some FAQs for your followers to see when they first land on your Facebook page. Though you can share pinned posts as many times as you want, you can only pin a single post at a time.

3. Facebook stories

You can now use Facebook stories to market your products. Facebook stories work in the same way as Instagram stories. They are a form of organic marketing and are only visible to your followers and page visitors. These stories are seen above your Facebook newsfeed and are fleeting images or videos that disappear after 24 hours. The video length of a Facebook story is 20 seconds and that of an image is five seconds. Facebook stories can now be included as an additional placement to News Feed or Instagram story ad campaigns. They are able to deliver your message in a fullscreen, immersive environment. A Facebook-commissioned survey found that 62% of people said they became more interested in a brand or product after seeing its products/services in a story.[69]

Facebook stories are customizable and provide an edge-to-edge experience that lets businesses immerse people in their content. Stories are optimized for a vertical, full-screen view that feels natural and allows people to enjoy videos and photos quickly. Comments and reactions to stories can only be seen by the the account owner. Stories are a great way to share live or timely information such as events, updates, etc. They also are helpful in engaging customers who may have missed any updates on the news feed and can be used to conduct polls, share breaking news, and run contests. While regular posts are displayed in the news feed, stories are displayed at the top of the user's Facebook page, making it more probable for users to view them as soon as they open Facebook. Facebook stories are used by almost 500 million people every day and over 50% of people say that after seeing a brand story, they have visited a business's website to purchase a product or service.[70] Facebook stories can also be shared through Facebook Messenger.

4. Facebook groups

Facebook groups are a useful organic marketing tool that helps businesses attract new customers and engage current ones using specific content, community, and support. Facebook groups provide a place where one can find people who share similar interests, lifestyles, and needs. When such a group of

---

69. "Introducing Facebook Stories Ads," Meta for Business, September 26, 2018, https://en-gb.facebook.com/business/news/introducing-facebook-stories-ads.

70. Leah Golob, "How to Use Facebook Stories for Business: The Complete Guide," Social Media Marketing & Management Dashboard, July 5, 2023, https://blog.hootsuite.com/facebook-stories/.

people having similar or common shared interests, culture, nationalities, or purpose come together online, they become part of an online community, also known as a web community or internet community. Social media is one such platform where various online communities are formed, known as social media communities. The people in these communities share their experiences, ask questions, have discussions, give advice, and conduct various activities within the community.

A business can create a Facebook group and connect it to its page to build a community of fans and followers. The group's privacy settings can be customized, enabling the business to make the group private or public, i.e., the business can choose who can see and join their group.

Businesses must make the group more engaging by posting engaging content, leading discussions, hosting contests or live videos, etc. Many entrepreneurs and people have started Facebook groups and built them into a community of millions and generating revenue and business.

Examples: A Facebook page in Pune, India is one such example of a social media community. This group called Pune Eat Outs (PEO) boasts over 198,000 members, mainly from Pune city. The members are food lovers, food bloggers, and restaurant owners who keep sharing various posts related to eating out. So you will find posts such as restaurant reviews, food tasting reviews, food blogs, and customer reviews of various places they ate out at, along with offline meets, contests, and offers.

Some Interesting communities built on Facebook (Facebook Groups):

- **Makeup Artists:** with over 4.7 million members, this community helps makeup artists collaborate, share new ideas, learn new skills and trends, and network.

- **Instant Pot Community:** The 3.1 million users of this famous electric cooker brand use this group to ask questions, post recipes, get useful tips, and share their experiences.

- **Keto for Beginners:** A community of 1.6 million members for people who want to start the Keto diet. Users can address their queries to other members, share recipes, and guide other members in their diet journey towards fitness.

- **Girls LOVE Travel:** This is a global community of 1.3 million members who are women travelers. They use this community to provide resources and empowerment to each other and travel around the world.

FITTR is one such group on Facebook. Started by Jitendra Chouksey to keep people fit and help them build a fitness-centric lifestyle, it has over three million members who can connect to fitness and nutrition coaches and subscribe to various plans to lose weight or become fit. Those who do not wish to subscribe to any plans can read posts, share their thoughts, get their queries solved and questions answered, and find support. Many users share stories and pictures of their amazing transformations or weight loss journeys which act as an inspiration to other users. It has become the world's largest Community-First Fitness and Nutrition brand. Users share reviews of their coaches inspiring other users to enroll under them to achieve their own fitness goals.

***

Another example of a Facebook Group is **Instant Pot** which has close to 2.8 million members. This group is an example of a public group, where one needn't join to be able to see all the posts. The owners of Instant Pot electric cookers created this group in 2005 and since then it has grown. The group is used to share recipes, tips, and advice. Users of the product can get their queries resolved here and the company also uses this group to run giveaways so that they can build a database of email addresses and share their content and recipes.

5. Facebook Marketplace

Facebook is used by people to buy and sell from one another. In the previous point, we have discussed how Facebook Groups created for this purpose have grown substantially. Many people use these groups to buy and sell each month, including both small and large businesses.

Hence, Facebook introduced Marketplace to make the best of these connections and offer a place for buyers and sellers to meet and exchange their goods and services. Thus, Facebook Marketplace is a convenient destination for discovering, buying, and selling items with people from a community. Users can visit Marketplace by tapping on the shop icon at the bottom of the Facebook app. They can see photos of products listed for sale by people near them. Users can browse through the products using various filters, save items they like, and connect to the seller by seeing their name, profile description, location, and details about the product. Facebook doesn't provide the facility of paying for or delivering the products through this app. Once buyers and sellers connect, they can take it further from there on their own, in any way they choose. Facebook Marketplace does not charge any listing fees, unlike other such platforms and this makes it a channel for organic marketing.

5.1.2 Paid Marketing on Facebook

1. Facebook ads

Facebook allows you to create and run advertising campaigns with the help of simple self-serve tools. It also aids you in tracking the performance of these ads with easy-to-read reports. As over two billion people use Facebook each month, you are likely to find your target audience among this vast population.

You can follow this process for creating an ad on Facebook:

Figure 5.3 **Process for creating a Facebook ad**

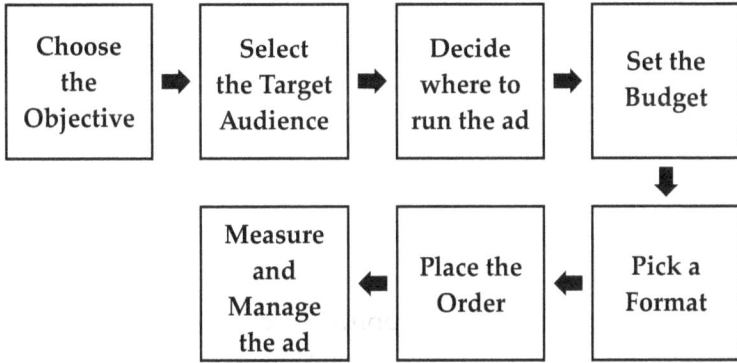

```
┌──────────┐    ┌──────────┐    ┌──────────┐    ┌──────────┐
│  Choose  │    │  Select  │    │  Decide  │    │ Set the  │
│   the    │ ▶  │the Target│ ▶  │ where to │ ▶  │  Budget  │
│Objective │    │ Audience │    │run the ad│    │          │
└──────────┘    └──────────┘    └──────────┘    └──────────┘
                                                      │
                                                      ▼
┌──────────┐    ┌──────────┐    ┌──────────┐
│ Measure  │    │          │    │          │
│   and    │ ◀  │Place the │ ◀  │ Pick a   │
│  Manage  │    │  Order   │    │ Format   │
│  the ad  │    │          │    │          │
└──────────┘    └──────────┘    └──────────┘
```

There are 8 kinds of Facebook ads:

Figure 5.4 **Types of Facebook ads**

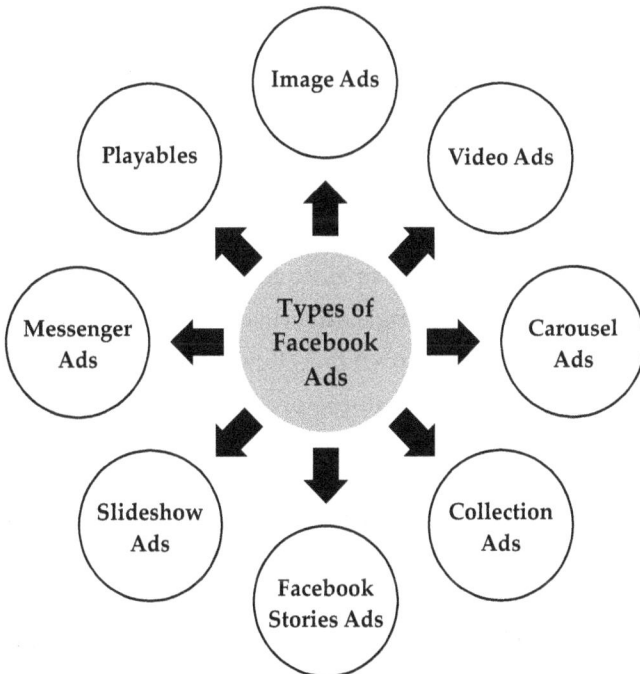

1. **Image ads**

   Static image ads, also known as single image ads feature a single image, headline, text, description text, and a call to action. Image ads are effective when the business wants to convey a single, straightforward message. These types of ads are ideal for driving traffic to the business's website.

2. **Video ads**

   When businesses want to showcase their product, build and increase brand awareness, or promote customer testimonials, video ads are a great option. Video posts have an engagement rate* of approximately 6.09% on Facebook, which is considered very good. However, businesses can lose viewers if the video quality is poor or has an unclear message. Video ads too have similar customization as single image ads.

   Facebook Reels are short videos that allow you to create entertaining short-form videos. Reel ads are built for mobile and help you reach your target audience in an entertaining manner and with a more immersive experience.

3. **Carousel ads**

   Carousel ads allow businesses to showcase up to 10 images or videos within a single advertisement, each image or video containing its own link. Businesses can use this format to highlight multiple products, tell their brand story, or showcase specific details about a particular product.

   Carousel ads are effective in educating the audience about the product or service, especially if the business has many different services to showcase or a few customer niches to appeal to. For example, a restaurant can showcase some of its most popular dishes, or an E-commerce site selling apparel could use multiple images to show the front, back (various angles), and close-up image of a dress.

4. **Collection ads**

A collection ad is showcased on Facebook News Feed. It consists of a cover video or image followed by three product images. When a user clicks on a collection ad, they see a full-screen landing page. This page can enable engagement and create interest and intent among the users.

Image collection ads are a great way to show products in an e-commerce store. However, just like image ads, there is a limitation of a short headline and a 125-character limit for the primary message, so businesses that wish to convey more information do not find them very suitable.

5. **Facebook story ads**

In September 2018, Facebook officially launched Facebook story ads for advertisers globally. Considering the large number of people using Facebook stories, it is a significant form of advertising. Facebook story ads, similar to Facebook stories, are vertical, visual ads that appear in the Stories Feed on mobile devices. Users can also swipe up to a "call-to-action" which redirects them to an external page, like your website or your product page on an e-commerce site. You can use text, images, and/or videos for your Facebook story ads.

Many brands such as KFC, Kettle Chips, iHeart, Levis, Adidas, Sephora, etc. have seen brand lift (how ads improve the perception of people towards your brand) from their Facebook story ads.

6. **Slideshow ads**

Facebook slideshow ads are video-like ads. Slideshow ads use motion, sound, and text to tell the business's story beautifully across various devices. They load quickly, hence they play well on every connection speed.

Slideshow ads are quick and affordable to create as compared to most video ads. Businesses can create a slideshow ad in a matter of minutes from their desktop or mobile and use it to tell a story that develops over time. They can even create a slideshow ad out of stock images available in the ad creation process, or use an existing video.[71]

7. **Messenger ads**

Messenger ads help customers start conversations with businesses and vice-versa. They add a personalized experience by promoting conversations and discussion and addressing individual queries. Facebook automatically delivers ads to the placement that is most likely to drive results from the campaign at the lowest possible cost. Businesses can use the same creative ads for Messenger that they're already using for Facebook and Instagram. Users see these ads in the Chats tab in their Messenger app. On tapping on an ad, they are redirected to a detailed view within Messenger with a call-to-action that will take them to the business' desired destination chosen during the creation of the ads; it could be the business' site, an app, or a conversation tab on Messenger with the business.

---

71. "Facebook Slideshow Ads," Meta for Business, n.d., https://en-gb.facebook.com/business/ads/slideshow-ad-format#.

8. **Playables**

Facebook playable ads give users a preview before they download an app. It is known as a try-before-you-buy experience. Playables are interactive video ads for the Facebook Audience network. It is primarily targeted towards mobile app developers who wish to advertise their apps on Facebook. Playable ads drive higher quality and higher-intent users to install apps after trying them. They create an immersive preview, allowing users to test-drive the app, and find engaged customers and players.

The above eight types of ads can be used individually or in combination to reach your target audience. The ad type to be chosen by a business depends mainly on its campaign goal. For example, if the business wants to employ a compelling Call-to-Action (CTA), an image ad would be the most effective, whereas if the business wants to engage audiences, videos or playables would be a better option.

Facebook ads have no set cost. Businesses bid on ad slots across the platform; the cost of the ad depends on how much the business is willing to pay to secure their preferred slot.

2. FBX (Facebook Exchange)

FBX is a proprietary platform owned by Facebook. It is an advertising service for desktop users. It uses a real-time bidding process for placing advertisements on the Facebook sidebar or onto users' timelines, which will be visible as they scroll down. As mentioned, it is primarily focused on desktop users and has hardly any functionalities for mobile apps. FBX, however, is not open to the general public. It is available only for very large advertisers, meaning that generally, most businesses need to be partnered with an online advertising agency to access FBX. It gives the advertiser prime real estate, i.e., a prime location for their advertisement. FBX ads are mainly targeted towards generating sales and getting conversions by driving more traffic to the company's website.

3. Audience Network ads

Now, people don't spend all their time on Facebook only; there are ample other social media apps that businesses need to leverage to reach their target audience. Hence, Facebook has come up with Audience Network which allows businesses to extend their advertising campaigns to other high-quality apps in order to reach more people. Research by Facebook has shown that conversion rates for people who saw ads across Facebook, Instagram, and Audience Network were eight times higher than people who saw the ads on Facebook. The targeting, auction, delivery, and measurement systems for Audience Network ads are the same as Facebook ads. Audience Network has image, video, and carousel ads.

4. Facebook influencer marketing

If you want to target newer, more niche, or different markets, marketing campaigns created by your central teams may not resonate with the target audience in these markets. For example,if you want to expand your market to Asia, marketing programmes that work in the USA may not necessarily succeed in Asian countries. To address this challenge, you must localize your content, so that it may resonate with the target audience. For this purpose, influencer marketing serves as an effective tool. Influencer marketing helps build brand awareness and drive sales. For example, you can identify the top influencers in the Asian countries you want to expand to and then include them in your social media marketing efforts. Due to its large user base, Facebook serves as a good platform for influencer marketing as you can reach a larger target audience. In 2022, Meta (Facebook's parent company) planned to invest almost $1 billion in programs that would benefit creators on its platform.[72] This would help creators earn more money for the content they create on Facebook as well as Instagram. To encourage creators to produce engaging, high-quality content on Facebook, Meta offers them up to $350,00, depending on the number of views they can generate from their Facebook Reels. You can find suitable influencers for your brand by searching for relevant hashtags, conducting surveys of existing followers, encouraging existing users to share their experiences, and searching for keywords using search engines.

Once the influencers are identified, you can collaborate with them so that they endorse your brands. You must then evaluate their content as well as the results of their marketing campaign to optimize your Facebook influencer marketing.

5.1.3 Cost of Facebook Advertising

Studies show that advertisers pay around $0.94 per click or $12.07 per 1,000 impressions.[73] Facebook bills advertisers based on two metrics: Cost per Click (CPC) and Cost per Mille (CPM) — otherwise known as cost per 1,000 impressions. The average CPC

---

72. Facebook Company and Meta, "Investing $1 Billion in Creators," Meta, July 14, 2021, https://about.fb.com/news/2021/07/investing-1-billion-dollars-in-creators/.

73. Sarah Berry, "How Much Does Facebook Advertising Cost in 2023?," WebFX, September 28, 2023, https://www.webfx.com/social-media/pricing/how-much-does-facebook-advertising-cost/.

for Facebook ads is $0.94, making it cheaper than advertising on LinkedIn, Instagram, or YouTube.

It is to be noted that the cost of a winning Facebook ad bid is affected by both seasonality and competition, especially since many advertisers desire website visits from the ads. Many online stores use Facebook for building brand awareness as Facebook has over 2.8 billion monthly active users, many of whom use it to engage with their favorite brands. Businesses that have goals of reach and awareness can be expected to pay around $12.07 to reach 1,000 people through Facebook.

(**Disclaimer:** Please note that pricing changes rapidly in the current dynamic marketing environment. The prices mentioned here aren't indicative of the current state and are for illustrative purposes only)

5.1.4 Facebook Ad Auctions

You should know how Facebook conducts its ad auction as this would help you to start optimizing your Facebook ad costs.

In a Facebook ad auction, the advertiser logs into the AD Manager to create an ad. They then choose their daily budget, i.e., the maximum amount they are willing to spend on each day. The advertiser selects the action they'll pay for, like views, clicks, or downloads, and builds their audience using interests, demographics, and device targeting. They then add their creative elements viz. the ad copy, images, videos, etc. following which, they approve and launch their ad.

Facebook uses an ad auction to determine the best ad to show to a person at a given time. The ad which wins the auction bid, provides maximum value for both businesses and people. Every time an ad can be shown to someone, an auction takes place to determine which ad should be shown to that user. Thus, there are billions of auctions taking place daily on various Facebook apps.

The ad that wins the Facebook ad auction is the one that provides the maximum value to both advertisers and the audience. This value includes a combination of three main factors:

- **Ad bid:** The amount that the advertiser is willing to pay to achieve his objectives.

- **Estimated action rate:** An estimate of whether the ad will result in action, i.e. will the person seeing the ad take the action desired by the advertiser?

- **Ad quality:** Ad quality is measured using various parameters such as feedback from the audience viewing or hiding the advertisement, assessment of low-quality parameters such as withheld information, engagement bait, and sensationalized language.

Action rates and ad quality, together, measure the ad relevance. A relevant ad could win a bid as opposed to expensive bids. Hence businesses must focus on making their ads more relevant by improving their quality and action rate.

5.2 Instagram Marketing

As we have seen in the previous chapters, Instagram is becoming one of the most popular social media platforms. Currently, it is the second most accessed social media network after Facebook. With more than one billion monthly users and over 500 million Instagram stories each day, it is an attractive medium for advertisers. According to research conducted by Statista, over 60% of Instagram users fall in the age group of 18 to 34.[74] It is a good way to target the youth who are increasingly using and spending time on Instagram. Instagram allows businesses of all types to select the ad format they wish to tell their brand story and market their brands.

Almost 90% of Instagram users follow at least one business and 83% of Instagram users have discovered a product/service on Instagram.[75] It is, thus, a good platform for introducing a business's new products or services and building brand awareness and brand loyalty through customer engagement.

---

74. Statista, "Instagram: Distribution of Global Audiences 2023, by Age Group," August 25, 2023, https://www.statista.com/statistics/325587/instagram-global-age-group/.

75. Statista, "Instagram: Distribution of Global Audiences 2023, by Age Group," August 25, 2023, https://www.statista.com/statistics/325587/instagram-global-age-group/.

You can market on Instagram in the following ways:

Figure 5.5   **Types of Instagram Marketing**

5.2.1 Organic Instagram Marketing

1. Photos

You can post photos or images to your Instagram account. These can include pictures of your products, brands, company, users, sales promotion offers, events, etc. Instagram provides filters or adjustments to edit your photos. These photos are visible only to those who visit your account or friends of those who may share these posts. So compared to photo ads, which are visible to a larger audience and not just to those visiting your page, they have a much lower reach and frequency.

2. Carousels

You can share a single post containing not more than ten photos to your Instagram Feed. This kind of post containing multiple photos is known as a carousel. Once shared, your account's followers can see the first photo or video from your post in their news feed.

3. Videos

Instagram allows you to share videos that your audience can watch and share. 91% of active Instagram survey respondents say they watch videos on Instagram weekly.[76] From July 2022, you can only share most videos as reels. Some videos aren't affected by this change, including videos previously posted to your feed and videos posted on Instagram web.[77]

4. Reels

Reels are short videos that can be shared with your audience to connect with them. Instagram Reels, which were launched in 2020, became Instagram's fastest-growing feature within a span of two years. Reels have amassed mass popularity for their entertaining content and short-length format, which help capture the audience's attention towards your brand. From 2022, new video posts that are under 15 minutes are shared as reels.[78] These

76. "Instagram Business Insights: Push Your Brand's Creativity," Instagram for Business, n.d., https://business.instagram.com/blog/instagram-business-insights-creativity?locale=en_GB.

77. "Record a Reel on Instagram | Instagram Help Center," n.d., https://help.instagram.com/2720958398006062.

78. "Video Content on Instagram Will Now Be Instagram Reels," Instagram for Business, n.d., https://business.instagram.com/blog/instagram-video-now-instagram-reels?locale=en_GB.

reels can be edited using various tools provided by Instagram. With reels, users get a full-screen and a more immersive experience. If the reel is under 90 seconds, it becomes eligible for recommendations from users, which will increase its reach and frequency, but it must be posted on a public account. What differentiates reels from stories is that they do not disappear after 24 hours and remain on Instagram until you delete them. What makes reels even better for marketing is Instagram's algorithm, which enables reels to reach people who are not your followers. Moreover, the algorithm tracks people's interests and shows them related content, which means there is an increased chance of your content reaching your target audience.

5. Stories

Instagram Stories allow you to share photos and videos with your users. These Stories are visible to your users for 24 hours after you publish them, after which they disappear, unless you have added them to your profile as story highlights. Instagram claims that 50% of Instagrammers have visited a website to buy a product or service after seeing it in Stories.[79] Stories are useful when you want to create quick and engaging content or reshare your existing posts and reels.

5.2.2 Paid Instagram Marketing

1. Photo ads

Photo ads on Instagram use single photos that can be placed on the Instagram Feed or Instagram Stories. Square, landscape, or

---

79. "Instagram Video Strategies for Ads," Instagram for Business, n.d., https://business. instagram.com/ad-solutions/video-strategy.

portrait photos are used in the photo ads. Photo ads feature a link to the product page or website. A Facebook study[80] showed that a series of photo-only advertisements were more effective than other ad formats in driving unique traffic to the product page/site. Photo ads are beneficial in creating product/brand awareness and are easier and less time-consuming to create.

2. Video ads

Videos of up to 60 minutes in length can be posted on Instagram to advertise a product/service. Instagram video ads can be placed in different manners, viz. Instagram video ads, story ads, sponsored reels, and feed video ads. These ads cost somewhere between 20 cents to $2 per click.[81] As Instagram is all about the visual experience, video ads not only provide this visual experience but add audio and effects to make it more appealing.

3. Reels ads

Instagram launched Reel ads in 2021 to help businesses reach larger audiences. Reels can be used by businesses to share immersive, interesting, and entertaining content in order to connect with the target audience. Reel ads are full-screen and vertical. While organic reels can be upto 90 seconds long, paid reels can be up to 60 seconds long. The audience can view, comment on, like, share, and save Reels. Reels are extremely popular with not just audiences but also businesses.

---

80. "Facebook Photo Ads," Meta for Business, n.d., https://www.facebook.com/business/ads/photo-ad-format.

81. Werner Geyser, "How Much Does It Cost to Advertise on Instagram?," Influencer Marketing Hub, June 8, 2022, https://influencermarketinghub.com/instagram-ads-cost/.

Reels can be used for generating leads, creating brand awareness, increasing sales, boosting your website traffic, customer engagement, building your brand reputation, and much more. You can use Instagram's editing tool for creating reels or you can also use popular software such as InShot, InVideo, Clips Adobe Rush, Canva, Splice, and a multitude of other options.

4. Carousel ads

These are similar to photo and video ads but instead of a single image or video, there are multiple images or videos, which users can browse through by swiping to view additional videos or images. With the help of carousel ads, businesses can showcase more products and services through multiple images and videos with a single ad. For example, when users scroll from right to left, you can show new apparel designs or different flavors of icecream. So in one ad, there may be 10 different products that users can browse through. As these ads contain multiple images, they are attractive and result in increased customer engagement.

5. Story ads

Story ads are intended to be fast, memorable, and fun. They are used for building awareness for the product/brand, driving traffic to the website, and tagging products to enable easy shopping from within the app itself. These short, fun, and immersive videos are well suited for fast-paced life and people with shorter attention spans, hence they are gaining popularity.

6. Ads in Explore

Ads in Explore is a function of Instagram ads targeted towards businesses wishing to advertise their products. Explore is a discovery surface on Instagram consisting of a collection of content that is based on the individual interests of a user. It sources content from across Instagram based on these interests. In order to access Explore, users need to click on the magnifying glass icon on their homepage of Instagram.

When users click on an image or video from Explore, they start seeing ads in their browsing experience. This is similar to an Instagram feed.

5.2.3 Cost of Instagram Ads

Due to its increasing popularity and emergence as the second most popular social media platform after Facebook, Instagram is being used increasingly by marketers to reach their target audience. Similar to Facebook, Instagram uses a bidding model to decide the cost of the ad to businesses. An Instagram ad costs anywhere between $0.20 to $2 for CPC ads and $6.70 for CPM ads. Advertisers are expected to pay around $.01 to $.05 dollars for CPE or Cost per Engagement.[82]

As compared to Facebook ads, Instagram ads cost less, i.e., almost half of the price paid for Facebook ads. Facebook has more users and businesses can reach users of all ages there, whereas Instagram is used to reach younger segments, mostly below 30 years of age.

---

82. Neil Patel, "How Much Do Instagram Ads Cost in 2023?," Neil Patel, August 28, 2021, https://neilpatel.com/blog/instagram-ads-prices/.

5.3 Threads Marketing

Meta's newest social media platform, launched in July 2023, is planning to introduce new marketing tools to attract brands. As you don't need to pay anything to join Threads, it is lucrative for marketers as it doesn't affect their marketing budgets. Currently, you can only do organic marketing on Threads. Marketers are unable to buy advertising space currently but Threads is working on creating opportunities for marketers to use paid ads to target their audiences.

To safeguard your business' social media presence, you can open a Threads account. You can organically market on Threads in the following ways:

1. By creating your profile and connecting to your target audience

2. Generating organic traffic

3. Creating exclusive threads for starting conversations about your brands

4. Collaborating with influencers to promote your brand and increase its popularity

5. Encouraging users to create and share content related to your products and brands

6. Motivating users to speak to other users about your brand, thus creating brand awareness and increasing your reach

As Mark Zuckerberg has said that he expects Threads to grow massively in the future, it can be expected that there will be many changes and new features added.

Quiz

1. For over 53% of internet users below the age of 24, what remains the primary source to research brands?

   a. E-commerce website

   b. Social media

   c. Company website

   d. Other informational websites

2. Which of the following is NOT a type of Facebook marketing?

   a. Page

   b. Groups

   c. Marketplace

   d. Ads in Explore

3. Facebook helps users track the performance of these ads with easy-to-read reports.

   a. True

   b. False

4. _____consists of a cover video or image followed by three product images.

   a. Carousel ads

   b. Image ads

   c. Collection ads

   d. None of the above

5. _____ allow businesses to showcase up to 10 images or videos within a single advertisement, each image or video containing its own link

   a. Carousel ads

   b. Image ads

   c. Collection ads

   d. None of the above

6. CPC stands for _____.

   a. Cost Per Click

   b. Cost Per Customer

   c. Cost Per Carousel

   d. Cost Per Contact

7. **CPM stands for _____.**

    a. Cost Per Message

    b. Cost Per Thousand

    c. Cost Per Measurement

    d. None of the above

8. **Every time an ad can be shown to someone, an auction takes place to determine which ad should be shown to that user.**

    a. True

    b. False

9. **FITTR and Instant Pot are examples of _____.**

    a. Facebook groups

    b. Facebook tools

    c. Facebook Auction tools

    d. None of the above.

10. **Users can visit _____ by tapping on the shop icon at the bottom of the Facebook app.**

    a. Facebook groups

    b. Facebook Business page

    c. Marketplace

    d. Facebook Live

Answers	1 – b	2 – d	3 – a	4 – c	5 – c
	6 – a	7 – b	8 – a	9 – a	10 – c

Chapter Summary

◆ The practice of promoting a brand or a business using Facebook is called Facebook marketing.

◆ Facebook marketing can be done in 2 ways: organic marketing and paid marketing.

◆ In organic marketing, you don't need to pay Facebook for running your ad. Organic Facebook marketing includes Facebook pages, Facebook Stories, Facebook Groups, and Marketplace.

◆ Paid marketing can be done through Facebook ads, influencer marketing, Facebook Exchange (FBX), and Audience Network Ads.

◆ There are 8 types of Facebook ads: image ads, video ads (including short videos called reels), carousel ads, collection ads, Facebook story ads, slideshow ads, Messenger ads, and playables.

◆ Facebook ads cost around $0.94 per click or $12.07 per 1,000 impressions. The cost is decided based on a bidding process.

◆ Instagram marketing is a good way to target the youth, especially those below 30 years of age.

◆ Instagram marketing has the following forms: photo ads, video ads, carousel ads, story ads, and ads in Explore.

◆ Instagram ads cost anywhere between $0.20 to $2 for CPC ads and $6.70 for CPM ads. Advertisers are expected to pay around $.01 to $.05 for CPE or Cost per Engagement.

This page is intentionally left blank

Chapter **6**

X (Formerly Twitter), LinkedIn, YouTube, and Pinterest Advertising and Marketing

X (Formerly Twitter), LinkedIn, YouTube, and Pinterest are also some of the major social media platforms used across the globe. They each have a distinct user base, allowing you to choose the right platform to reach your target audience more effectively. This chapter discusses the characteristics of each of these platforms while explaining how to use them for marketing.

The key learning objectives should include the reader's understanding of the following:

- How do we use X (Formerly Twitter), LinkedIn, YouTube, and Pinterest for marketing?

- How do we use Facebook and Instagram for advertising?

- What are the characteristics of each of these social media platforms?

- Which target audience can be reached using these media?

- How to Pin on Pinterest?

- What is the process of creating and uploading videos?

- What are hashtags and why are they used?

6.1 Twitter (now X) Marketing

Twitter, now rebranded as X, is among the top social media sites in not just the US but also the world. X marketing is aimed at improving traffic and engagement and building community interest in their product or service as well as generating sales. With around 238 million global monetizable Daily Active Users (mDAU), X has a large reach, which helps companies connect to a large number of prospective customers globally.

X marketing helps in:

a. creating awareness of the brand or product

b. driving more traffic to the company's website

c. customer engagement, with customers sharing Tweets (now called "posts"), replying, addressing queries and getting feedback

    d. building relationships with customers as you can share your thoughts, opinions, plans, etc. with customers, take their inputs and feedback, and have conversations with them

    e. understanding your target audience's behavior, likes, dislikes, needs, and expectations

    f. generating sales using X advertising and marketing your products and services to the target audience, who can be converted into customers

    g. building and maintaining a community of the brand's followers and fans who support your business.

6.1.1 Organic Marketing on X

Organic marketing on X includes the tweets (now "posts") you share from your X profile page. These posts will be visible to all your followers and people who visit your page. You can post text, GIFs, images, and videos. You can use hashtags which will help in increasing the reach of your post to those who search for those keywords, thus effectively reaching prospects. A lot of organic search traffic gets directed to X and your posts can be seen by such users. Unlike Facebook and Instagram, most X users are older, with their median age being around 40 years. A large percentage (42%) of X users have college degrees.[83] Thus, you need to keep these demographics in mind when targeting an audience on X.

Organic X marketing does have certain limitations. Due to the extremely large number of posts being sent out per minute, posts may get crowded. Moreover, posts are displayed chronologically.

---

83. Brock Andony, "Organic Twitter Marketing: The Fundamental Guide - Vendasta Blog," Vendasta Blog, April 29, 2022, https://www.vendasta.com/blog/organic-twitter-marketing/.

Your post can get lost in this crowd or may get overshadowed by more recent tweets. If you have a limited number of followers or limited search traffic being directed to your page, you will need to supplement your organic marketing with paid marketing.

6.1.2 Paid Marketing on X

Paid marketing on X mainly consists of advertising. There are 5 kinds of paid ads on X:

1. Promoted ads

These ads are clearly marked with a "Promoted" icon in the lower left corner to let users know that they are paid ads. **Promoted ads** are ordinary posts purchased by advertisers who want to reach a wider group of users or spark engagement from their existing followers.[84] You need to pay for the placement of these ads on X. These promoted ads have the same features as ordinary tweets, which means you can retweet, follow, like, or comment on them. Promoted ads may include text ads, image ads, video ads, and carousel ads.

2. Amplify ads

Amplify Pre-roll, also known as amplify ads help creators monetize videos. X allows you to post videos of up to 10 minutes along with tweets. Amplify Pre-roll pair pre-roll (an online video advertisement that plays before the start of a video) from advertisers with premium, brand-safe video content on X using the chosen tags for each video. You can easily opt-in for your videos to become a part of the revenue share program. You

---

84. "What Are Promoted Ads?," n.d., https://business.twitter.com/en/help/overview/what-are-promoted-ads.html.

can also choose which videos to monetize and amplify high-performing videos to reach wider audiences. You can select the content categories of the videos that your video ad will be served on. There are over 15 categories to select from. Amplify sponsorships give you a 1:1 pairing with a publisher at a moment of your choice. You are also given tweet-level control during the campaign.[85]

3. X Takeover ads

X Takeover ads are the most premium, mass-reaching placements that drive results across the spectrum by taking over the Timeline and Explore tabs. They give brands exclusive ownership of X's premium real estate across desktop and mobile, allowing you to maximize reach and drive lifts. [86] There are 2 ways these ads are offered:

1. Trend Takeover seamlessly positions your advertisement within the trending topics on X's Explore tab, providing businesses with a high-impact 24-hour dominance of both the top Trends list on X and the Explore tab on mobile, the go-to destination for real-time updates. Additionally, you can opt for Trend Takeover+ to enhance your advertisement message with immersive video creative.

2. Timeline Takeover ensures your brand takes the lead in conversations by being the first ad of the day. With Timeline Takeover, your ad becomes one of the initial things people see upon opening X.

---

85. "X Ad Formats," n.d., https://business.twitter.com/en/advertising/formats. html#amplify-twitter.

86. "Trend Takeovers," n.d., https://business.twitter.com/en/advertising/takeover/trend-takeovers.html.

4. X Live

Using X Live, advertisers can broadcast their most important moments to the world and allow audiences to join in real-time. They can broadcast product launches, conferences, watch parties, etc. . With the help of X Live, brands maximize their reach as well as drive conversation with their target audiences.

5. Dynamic product ads

Using Dynamic Product Ads (DPA), you can deliver the most relevant product to the right customer at the right time. DPA Re-targeting helps you direct ads toward consumers who have engaged with your products. For example, it can cater to consumers who may have added one of your products to their shopping cart but have not completed the purchase transaction. DPA Prospecting helps you acquire new customers who have not visited your website by showing them ads that feature products from your catalog.

6. Collection ads

Collection ads are a new way through which users can browse and buy products. You can use Collection ads to showcase a collection of product images through a primary hero image and smaller thumbnail visuals below. Unlike carousel ads where users need to swipe through individual cards, collection ads display all product features in a single view. You also have the option of linking your ads to unique product destinations and landing pages. You also get a larger creative space where you can showcase six unique products, services, or promotions.

7. Cost of X advertisements

X advertising costs* vary based on the type of advertisement, which includes promoted posts, promoted accounts, and promoted trends. It all functions using the bidding model, where you bid based on how much you're willing to pay per new customer.

- Promoted posts vary in cost, typically ranging from $0.50 to $2.00 per action based on bidding. These are your original timeline posts repurposed as sponsored content, appearing in the timelines of individuals who aren't following you.

- Promoted accounts, on the other hand, cost between $2 and $4 per follower. Promoted accounts are paid ads that promote your entire account. Users who do not follow you see a promoted tweet that features your account.

- Promoted trends, priced at $200,000 per day, are the priciest option among the three. They cater to larger businesses with extensive social media marketing budgets rather than small or medium-sized enterprises. Within the X newsfeed, the left-hand side bar titled "Trends for you" showcases current hashtags and topics trending on X, with Promoted trends securing the topmost position. To denote their status as paid content, X labels them with the term "Promoted."

6.1.3 How Do Businesses Use X for Marketing?

A well-crafted X marketing strategy can enhance sales, elevate brand awareness, and foster customer loyalty.

Following are the steps to be followed by businesses for marketing their products on X:

1. Conducting an X audit

You must create an X account if you don't have one already. If you do have an account, you need to analyze your profile, all the X accounts that you operate, the kind of content you have shared, how often you post, how many followers you have, how many followers are actively following you, which content was successful and which wasn't, etc.

The X Analytics dashboard is one such tool that helps businesses identify what is and isn't working for their profile and what can be done to improve it. An audit is beneficial in letting you know where your company stands and identify problems or areas of improvement.

2. Researching the target audience

Once the audit has been completed, you must identify your target audience and research their behavior on X. You must find out how many people visit and follow brand pages on X, how much time the audience spends on X, how frequently they visit, and what kinds of messages and accounts are more popular. Once you understand your audience's behavior on X, it will help you frame your X marketing strategies. You can use various tools such as X Analytics which helps you see other pages liked by your followers, what age groups the followers belong to and their occupations. Another tool that you can use is Twitonomy which shows the engagement statistics for other accounts (your competitors).

3. Setting X marketing objectives

Once the audit is completed and the target audience and their behavior are researched, it's essential to establish specific marketing objectives tailored to your X account. These goals should align with your overall objectives, such as increasing website traffic, engaging customers to boost brand awareness and loyalty, informing audiences about promotions, complementing advertising across other social media platforms, enhancing Click-Through Rates (CTR), and more. Ensure these objectives are realistic, clearly defined, achievable, and relevant to your business.

4. Creating a branded and customized X profile

You must create an X Profile that is aligned with your brand and target audience. Your X profile should contain the brand name, logo, colors, and any other details that the audience will remember and relate to the brand. The following parts of the X profile can be customized:

X Handle: The X handle of the business is nothing but your username. For example, @McDonalds or @kfc. The X handle should include the company's name to enable the customers, fans, and followers to easily search for the brand's official page on X. The X handle is created when one signs up to create an X account.

Header: The header is your background image visible on your X profile. You can use an image of your product, brand, logo, punch line, or advertisements as your header. For example, KFC's header shows a picture of their products with their tagline.

CTR is calculated as the total link clicks divided by impressions, expressed as a percentage.

X Profile Picture: A profile picture is displayed with every post, interaction, reply, and action on X. Positioned just above the business's bio, this image commonly features the company's logo, brand name, initials, or the founders/CEOs.

X Bio: Your X bio offers a concise 160-character summary for profile visitors. It can encompass your vision or mission statement, a brief company description, or something compelling, humorous, and engaging to captivate the audience.

Website URL: X provides the option of inserting a website's URL below the profile picture and bio. You can benefit a lot from this as this helps in directing traffic directly to your website.

Birthday: Along with the URL, you can also insert your company's birthday or foundation day. This helps the audience to get to know your brand more personally.

5. Carrying out X marketing activities

Once your custom X profile is set up, you can start marketing, using both free and paid methods. Decide who on your team will manage the account, post messages, and reply to people. On X, it's important to check often for new tweets and messages so you don't miss anything important and can reply quickly.

You should also establish a social media calendar or X schedule for planning tweet timings. Key events such as festivals, national days, and special occasions like Valentine's Day, birthdays, or anniversaries merit particular attention. These moments present great opportunities to launch offers and engage with your target audience. For instance, offering Valentine's Day discounts or free gifts to couples purchasing your products or services could be a valuable promotion.

You can also host an X chat to discuss a relevant topic, engage your fans and followers, or create a feeling of community. You need to select a particular date and time, topic, and hashtag for the event. This can then be shared through a tweet, on your X bio, as well as your website and anywhere else you wish to.

6. Evaluating the X marketing program and measuring its impact

You must regularly evaluate your X marketing program to check if your goals are being achieved. You must check the progress you have made against the goals set, and take corrective action wherever needed. You also need to evaluate these achievements carefully. For example, a particular advertisement or message may have been retweeted multiple times, but did it convert into sales? You can use various metrics and tools to measure the impact of your X marketing program. This is a crucial step for marketers as it will help you understand whether you are utilizing your time, money, and effort effectively. You can use the following process to evaluate your X marketing program:

a. Using analytics tools

You can use analytical tools to measure the effectiveness of your X marketing activities. X Analytics displays the key metrics which can be accessed by clicking on "Analytics" on your X homepage. It shows your profile visits, new/lost followers, impressions, re-tweets, engagement rate, top Tweet, top mention, top follower, link clicks, likes, replies, and much more. There is also a conversion tracking page that helps you calculate how many conversions took place in a given period. Additionally, there are many more tools such as Google Analytics, Tweepsmap, Twitonomy, Hootsuite, Buffer, Klear, etc.

b. Tracking the right metrics

You need to identify the metrics you need to track to gauge the effectiveness of your marketing activities. Following are a few of the metrics for your X marketing program:

- **Impressions:** How many people saw your content on their X feed?

- **Engagement:** How many times has the audience interacted in any way with any of your posts?

- **Activity Dashboard:** How have your posts performed over the last month? The activity dashboard helps you compare the current month's results with previous month.

- **X Followers Month-on-Month Growth:** How many followers do you have? How many followers did you have in the previous month and how many new followers have been added in the current month? It is important to know your followers' demographics, interests, and location. X analytics dashboard helps you see how many followers you have, their age, gender, area of residence, income level, and their interests.

- **Top Post:** X shows you your top post every month, which helps you understand what type of content works well for the audience. It is identified based on the number of impressions it has received over a period of 28 days.

c. Social listening

Social listening means that you must pay close attention to what is being said on X. Listening or paying attention to conversations that take place on X helps you gain a better understanding of your customers and competitors. You can identify both positive and negative things being written about you, and address them as required. You must pay attention to mentions of your business name, industry topics, competitors, trending topics, and buzzwords. You can use various tools to track this information. It can then be used to strengthen your messages, build brand loyalty and trust, improve problem areas, etc.

d. Measuring the impact

Once you have collected all the required data such as engagement rate, number of followers, mentions, growth, and so on, it helps you measure the impact of your X marketing campaign. It helps you understand if your strategy is effective or needs refinement. This is done by analyzing the data to determine whether objectives have been achieved. For example, if your objective was to increase website traffic, you will collect data on the number of visitors before, during, and after your Twitter marketing campaign and compare it to understand whether the campaign was effective in driving website traffic. This helps in designing future marketing campaigns.

6.1.4 Implications of Elon Musk's Takeover of Twitter

Twitter has been in the news since Elon Musk acquired the company and became the owner and CEO of Twitter on October 27, 2022. This change has huge implications for Twitter as many drastic changes were undertaken after this acquisition.

On June 5, 2023, Linda Yaccarino was appointed as the CEO of Twitter, while Musk transitioned to being executive chair and CTO. On July 22, 2023, Twitter was officially rebranded as "X".

That this change will have implications on marketing is certain.

Nicole Farley[87] says that due to trust and safety concerns under Musk's leadership, some agencies are advising that their clients suspend their ads on X, at least for now. One such advertising company is IPG's Mediabrands. The automaker and Tesla competitor GM temporarily paused their ads, while stating that they have temporarily paused their paid advertising. They further stated that they had not abandoned the platform completely and would continue customer care interactions on it.

A few of the many changes that have taken place after Elon Musk's takeover are as follows:

- Users now need to have an account and be logged in to view user profiles and tweets.

- Users have to pay $8 a month and businesses have to pay $1000 a month for Twitter Blue, where user profiles have a blue tick to verify their accounts.

- Accounts that link to rival platforms such as Facebook, Instagram, etc. would be removed.

- Twitter's Newsfeed — the collection of Tweets that users see when they open the app — earlier only showed Tweets from accounts that the user followed. But now the feed is divided into two parts: "For You" which shows Tweets from accounts that the user doesn't follow along with new topics and interests; and a "Following" tab which users need to switch to if they want to see Tweets from followed accounts.

- There is now a limit on the number of posts that users can read in a day. While verified accounts can read not more than 6000 posts per day, unverified accounts are limited to

---

87. Nicole Farley, "How Brands and Agencies Are Reacting to Elon Musk's Radical Changes at Twitter," Search Engine Land, November 17, 2022, https://searchengineland.com/twitter-advertising-elon-musk-brands-agencies-389311.

reading 600 posts per day and new unverified accounts can read up to 300 posts per day.

- Earlier only likes, retweets, and replies were seen below the Tweets. Now, tweets are accompanied by various metrics such as the number of views the tweet has garnered and the number of times the tweet has been bookmarked and saved.

It remains to be seen whether X can regain lost advertisers and users by making changes or will continue to lose advertisers and users.

6.2 LinkedIn Marketing

LinkedIn is considered a significant tool in B2B Marketing. With a registered user size of over 830 million, more than 310 million active daily users, and 180 million senior-level executives, LinkedIn provides businesses with target audiences of business decision-makers. Four out of five LinkedIn members drive business decisions.[88] LinkedIn Marketing helps businesses by generating leads, driving their website traffic, and building brand awareness through LinkedIn ads.

LinkedIn Marketing is done in two ways:

1. **Starting a free Company LinkedIn Page: Organic Marketing**
   The LinkedIn page acts as the central hub for your business to post and share your updates. More than 57 million

---

88. Growleady, "'4 out of 5 Users on LinkedIn Drive Business Decisions' - What Does This Mean for Marketers and How Can You Make the Most out of It in Your Outreach?," December 15, 2021, https://www.linkedin.com/pulse/4-out-5-users-linkedin-drive-business-decisions-what-does-/.

businesses have a page on LinkedIn.[89]

Using LinkedIn you can connect with your target audience by sharing posts, PPTs, PDFs, Word Docs, etc. You can react, comment, and connect with your target audience and build a community of followers.

2. **Using LinkedIn Ads: Paid Marketing**

   LinkedIn ads are a good way of achieving your marketing objectives and driving brand awareness. There are many types of ads from which businesses can select the most suitable ones:

   - **Sponsored Content**

     Sponsored content is also known as native advertisement on LinkedIn. It can be used to reach and engage a professional audience. Sponsored content has image ads, video ads, document ads, carousel ads, and event ads. Sponsored content is used to share thought leadership, market products/services, and promote upcoming events. Businesses can sign in to Campaign Manager to create a sponsored marketing content plan, and personalize and test ads for native audiences as well as collect leads.

   - **Sponsored Messaging**

     Sponsored messaging is an informational or promotional native ad that is displayed for LinkedIn's partners as part of a marketing or hiring campaign. It is not sent to a personal or professional inbox, instead, it is only displayed on a member's LinkedIn Messaging web

---

89. "Create a LinkedIn Page | LinkedIn Marketing Solutions," Create a LinkedIn Page | LinkedIn Marketing Solutions, n.d., https://business.linkedin.com/marketing-solutions/cx/22/02/linkedin-pages-sr-d.

page or LinkedIn mobile app experience.[90] Sponsored messaging have two formats: LinkedIn Message ads, which can be used to send direct messages to prospects with the objective of sparking immediate action and **LinkedIn Conversation ads** which can be used to start conversations with businesses and professionals using LinkedIn Messaging on desktop as well as mobile devices.

- **Dynamic Ads**
  Dynamic ads are used to engage prospective customers through ads that are automatically personalized for them. Using Dynamic ads, you can build deeper relationships with your audience as the ads are automatically customized using publicly available information from LinkedIn member profiles, such as their profile photo, company name, or job title.[91]

- **Text Ads**
  Text ads are used to drive new customers to the business. They are suitable for those working on a budget as LinkedIn provides various options with its easy, self-service pay-per-click (PPC) advertising platform.[92] Text ads are simple ads visible on the top or right-hand side of the LinkedIn desktop feed.

---

90. "Opt out of Sponsored Messaging | LinkedIn Help," n.d., https://www.linkedin.com/help/linkedin/answer/62649/opt-out-of-sponsored-messaging#:~:text=LinkedIn%20Sponsored%20Messaging%20is%3A,personal%20or%20professional%20email%20inbox.

91. John Hayden, "LinkedIn Dynamic Ads Are Now Available In Campaign Manager," Digital Marketing Community, February 4, 2019, https://www.digitalmarketingcommunity.com/news/linkedin-dynamic-ads-are-now-available-in-campaign-manager/.

92. "Text Ads - Targeted Self-Service PPC & CPM Ads | LinkedIn Marketing Solutions," PPC Ads: Text Ads With LinkedIn PPC | LinkedIn Marketing Solutions, n.d., https://business.linkedin.com/marketing-solutions/ppc-advertising.

Figure 6.3 | **Why B2B Marketers should use LinkedIn:**

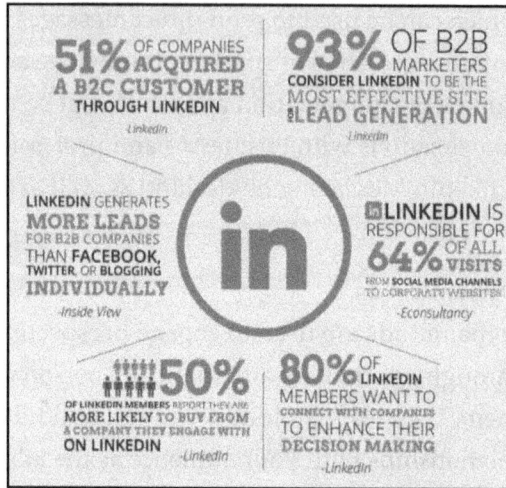

6.2.1 Cost of LinkedIn Advertisements

Like other social media platforms that we have seen so far, LinkedIn also operates on a bidding model in which businesses bid against other advertisers targeting the same audience. The cost of the advertisement depends on the bid along with the desirability of the target audience. A very important factor that influences the advertising costs on LinkedIn is the Ad Relevance score. The higher the Ad Relevance score, the lower the advertising cost, as LinkedIn aims to share engaging and relevant ads with its users.

The cost of LinkedIn ads* depends on the objectives which the business wants to attain, which audience they want to target, and how much competitors are willing to pay to reach the same audience. The CPC for LinkedIn ads starts at a minimum of $2 but the average CPC is around $8 to $11 per click and the CPM is around $33.80 per 1000 impressions.[93]

6.3 YouTube Marketing

YouTube is the second most visited website in the world, with over 2 billion people logging into it each month. This makes YouTube appealing to businesses for marketing their product to a huge audience. It is also notable that over 68% of active internet users have said that watching YouTube videos has helped them make a purchase decision. YouTube can also improve the SEO and brand awareness for your business.

Another reason that YouTube is considered a powerful marketing tool is that it has videos, and videos are a much more effective medium as compared to images or text. They make the message more interesting, capture the attention of the audience, and are more memorable. Moreover, businesses seeking localization find YouTube a very good option because it is available in over 100 countries and more than 80 languages. YouTube is the world's second most popular channel for businesses to share their video content, just after Facebook.[94]

However, a very small percentage of all small businesses in the US use YouTube according to Brandwatch.[95] This may be because producing videos is a tedious activity and is also expensive for

---

93. WebFX Team, "How Much Does LinkedIn Advertising Cost in 2023?," WebFX, September 28, 2023, https://www.webfx.com/social-media/pricing/how-much-does-linkedin-advertising-cost/.

94. Maryam Mohsin, "10 YouTube Statistics That You Need to Know in 2023," Oberlo (blog), July 20, 2023, https://www.oberlo.com/blog/youtube-statistics.

95. Loc. cit.

small businesses. However, you use free video editing software and stock video websites. Today, one can also use smartphones to shoot high-quality videos, which makes it easier for even small businesses to create videos.

YouTube is a very competitive place. If you think that you can just start uploading videos and see results, it isn't that simple. You may end up getting very few views and even fewer subscribers. To succeed on YouTube, create a strong strategy, craft quality videos, and learn about SEO to optimize content with keywords and topics that engage viewers.

YouTube launched YouTube Shorts in 2021 globally . YouTube Shorts is a short version of YouTube videos, where you can upload vertical videos that are not more than 60 seconds long. They are viewed in portrait mode. YouTube allows you to use its various built-in creation tools to create, edit, add music, text, and animations, control the speed, and edit various videos together to share on YouTube Shorts. YouTube Shorts might help you convert your viewers into subscribers. YouTube Shorts are a great way to promote your channel, increase your subscriber base, generate engagement, and launch teasers of your marketing videos.

6.3.1 How to Market on YouTube?

You can market your products or services organically on YouTube in the following ways:

Creating original videos

As YouTube is mainly a video-sharing platform, you can market your products or services effectively by creating and publishing high-quality videos designed to increase watch time. To create effective videos, you must follow the following steps:

1. **Research your topic:** What kinds of videos can be made around your topic? What kinds of videos have been shared by competitors? What is the duration of such videos?

2. **Set the objectives:** Do you want to educate, entertain, or create awareness? What is your budget? What will be the content of the video? What do you expect as its outcome –- views, website traffic, or sales?

3. **Prepare for the video:** What is the length you have decided for the video? Where do you want the video to be filmed? How many people do you need? Do you need vocals? Do you have the required equipment/gear such as a camera/webcam/smartphone, microphone, tripod, storage, lighting, etc.? Do you have screen recording software, video editing software, etc.? Do you have a script? Do you need to include any text or graphics in the video? Who will edit the video?

4. **Ensure high quality:** For creating a high-quality video you need: good resolution, format, aspect ratio, and video image size. You can choose from a wide range of resolutions such as 240p (426 x 240) to 2160p (3840 x 2160), known as 4K resolution. As the number of pixels keeps increasing, the video keeps getting sharper. You also need to select the format next. There are various types of formats such as MOV, MPMOV, MPEG-1, MPEG-2, MPEG-3, MPEG4, MP4, AVI, WMV, etc. A few formats such as MP3, WAV, etc. are not uploadable on YouTube and may need to be converted using software tools to be uploaded. Next is the aspect ratio, which denotes the proportional relationship between the width and height of the video. 16:9 is the most commonly used aspect ratio on YouTube.

5. **Record the video:** Check the lighting and background, set up the equipment, and record the video. You may need to re-record in case of mistakes or disturbances.

6. **Edit the video:** Once the video has been shot, you will need to edit it by organizing the clips, cutting out unnecessary parts, adding voice-over, adding transitions, adjusting the brightness, contrast, colors, etc., and adding text or imagery for the audience to read wherever needed. You can use video-editing software for this, or outsource to a video editor.

7. **Find the right keywords:** You need to use the right keywords which will help you optimize your video for search engines and reach your target audience effectively. Your keywords should appear in your title, description, thumbnails, and tags.

8. **Create a video title and thumbnail:** This is an extremely important step as your audience will first see the title and thumbnail hence it must be catchy, garner interest, and induce your audience to watch the video.

9. **Upload the Video:** You can finally upload your video by selecting the video icon on your YouTube page. You need to select the file you wish to upload, select your thumbnail, select your audience by stating whether it is suitable for kids or needs age restrictions, adhere to copyright instructions, select the privacy level, and publish the video.

You can run paid marketing campaigns on YouTube in the following ways:

1. Running videos

Studies have shown that more than 70% of users have bought products after seeing a YouTube ad or video and hence running video ads is a good way of creating brand awareness, increasing sales, and creating brand loyalty. You can generate high returns by running video ads on YouTube.

The cost of YouTube Ads* depends on the number of views. Each view costs between $0.10 to $0.30, depending on the target keywords and industry. The average cost to reach 100,000 viewers is approximately $2000.

2. Partnering with influencers

Influencers are also known as content creators. They have a huge number of subscribers who follow and trust them. Using influencers is a good option for you as it helps the brand reach a larger audience and since it comes from a trustworthy and eminently followed source, customers are more likely to trust and be influenced to buy the product or service. However, influencer marketing can be very expensive as influencers that have a larger number of followers and high engagement rates charge higher rates for their services. This may, therefore not be suitable for small businesses with limited marketing budgets.

6.3.2 Process of creating and uploading videos on YouTube

Videos can be created and uploaded on YouTube easily. Follow this process to create and upload videos on YouTube.

1. Decide the YouTube video marketing strategy

You must first decide your YouTube marketing strategy by deciding the objectives of YouTube marketing, such as creating brand awareness, increasing followers/subscriptions, getting maximum views, generating website traffic, increasing sales, and so on. You must also clearly define who your target audience is so that the videos will be aligned with them and be more effective.

2. Make the video SEO-Friendly

You must ensure that you consider Search Engine Optimization (SEO) for your video. The video content should be relevant to the audience and good enough to attract views. You should research the latest trends, topics that are most talked about, etc. while making the video and deciding its title and keywords.

3. Record and save the video

While recording the video you should check which formats are supported on YouTube such as MOV, MP4, AVI, WMV, MPEG4, and many more. You should ensure that you have good recording equipment which will result in high-quality videos. There are many equipment and online tools available which help create very good quality videos. Videos can be edited to improve the brightness, add music, cut unnecessary parts, add animation, etc.

4. Upload the video to YouTube

To upload the video to YouTube, you must log in to your YouTube account and click on the video icon which is shown at the top right-hand side of the window. Then you must click on "Upload a Video" and then select the files from those saved on the device. You can then choose to immediately publish the video or do so on a scheduled date and time of your choice.

5. Do the final detailing

You must select the privacy settings to control who can or cannot see the video. A video's privacy can be set to any of the three options: Public- in which the video can be seen by anyone and is the best option if you want to expand its reach; Unlisted- in which the video still remains public, but the video does not appear in YouTube search results or feeds, or Private: in which the video can be seen only by the user logged into the business account and not by anyone else.

6.4 Pinterest Marketing

With around 433 million users worldwide, Pinterest has emerged as an important marketing tool for businesses wishing. Moreover, research has shown that more than 83% of Pinterest users (Pinners) have made a purchase based on brand content they saw on Pinterest.[96] It is important to note that most of Pinterest's users are women (Around 60%) and hence, it is very suitable for businesses targeting the female segment of customers. With 40% of the user base consisting of men, marketers can target the male segment too.

To begin, you must start your own Pinterest account, which is free. Businesses get access to special content formats, custom analytics, and much more.[97] Pinterest offers meaningful engagement by creating a community of people who share similar

---

96. Pinterest. "Feed Optimization Playbook." n.d. https://assets.ctfassets.net/ h67z7i6sbjau/3IY6IiM0GhGeEYVIz3Tjnc/58cb4970482cfe9cc7f48dfb41e88123/Feed_ optimization_guide_2021.pdf

97. "Pinterest For Business: How to Market Your Brand \ | Pinterest Business," Pinterest, n.d., https://business.pinterest.com/en-in/.

passions. Choosing a business account as opposed to a personal account on Pinterest allows you to gain access to Pinterest Analytics as well as other features such as a native video player, a visual search tool, and the ability to run Pinterest ads.

Most Pinterest users look for and prefer visual content. Hence, Pinterest has become a very strong platform for distributing various kinds of content, including written blogs. On Pinterest, content is shared on Pinterest boards. Pins are created and saved on these boards and content is distributed for followers to explore. You can create as many boards as you want. They can further be organized into ideas, themes, plans, etc. to make it convenient for the audience to find what they're looking for. In fact, people such as existing customers or leads can be invited to join the boards to form a "group board" which is a great way of increasing engagement and interaction on your profile.

As with all other social marketing platforms, on Pinterest, too, you can market your products/brand organically or via paid advertising. Here's how you can organically market on Pinterest:

1. Creating a Pinterest business account

A Pinterest personal account does not offer all the benefits and features that a Pinterest business account does. So, if you want to utilize Pinterest for your marketing needs, you must first create a business account. The account should then be linked to any or all of your other social media accounts. Adding a Pinterest tag to your website will also help in tracking the number of visitors.

2. Displaying the brand on the profile page

Think of your Pinterest account just like your website and other social media. Make sure your brand image, logo, and product are clear in the cover, profile, and pins. This way, people easily recognize and remember your brand.

3. Identifying the target audience

You must identify your target audience so that the content can be created accordingly. Knowing the target audience is important as you can identify their problems and then customize solutions for them or demonstrate how the product or service will help in solving their problem. To identify the target audience on Pinterest, you can conduct keyword research, create boards, and start pinning content from your website such as your products, services, promotional offers, achievements, advertisements, and so on. Pinning more captivating and engaging content enhances its effectiveness in engaging the target audience and achieving marketing objectives. You must be consistent and regular in pinning and staying updated and connected to your target audience.

6.4.1 Paid marketing on Pinterest: Pinterest ads

According to Pinterest, their ads earn a 2x higher return on ad spend for retail brands compared to other social media and with a 2.3x cheaper cost per conversion, compared to other social media platforms.[98]

---

98. "Advertising on Pinterest | Pinterest Business," Pinterest, n.d., https://business.pinterest.com/en-in/advertise/.

Pinterest ads have 4 formats:

1. Standard ads

You can showcase your products and content in a simple vertical or square image format. They are similar to standard pins but they will have the word "promoted" next to them.

2. Video ads

You can capture attention and share stories using Pinterest's visually engaging video format. Video ads are ideal for sharing the brand story or garnering the interest of the audience. Video ads are available in both standard width and max-width formats. Standard video is the same size as regular Pins, while max width spans two columns on mobile.[99]

3. Carousel ads

Carousel ads allow users to swipe through multiple images in a single ad using their mobile phones or desktops. A carousel ad can be discerned using the three dots below the image. A single carousel ad can have 2-5 images. A user can save the entire carousel to their board, which can help them to refer to it when they want to make their purchase decision.

4. Collection ads

These are ads of a hybrid format through which you can display your products using mixed lifestyle imagery and video. They are displayed to mobile phone users and consist of a large

---

99. "Video Ads," Pinterest Help, n.d., https://help.pinterest.com/en/business/article/ promoted-video-with-autoplay

featured image or video accompanied by three supporting images. Another important feature of collection ads is that Pinterest can automatically create these ads for you by choosing related products from your catalog.

Cost of Pinterest ads

Cost Per Click (CPC)-- $0.00 - $0.10

Cost Per Thousand impressions (CPM)-- $0.00 - $1.50

Cost Per Conversion-- $0.00 - $2.00

On average, 59% small-to-medium-sized businesses (SMBs) spend between $0 to $500 per month on Pinterest ads and 19% businesses spend more than $5000 per month on Pinterest ads.[100]

6.5 Using Hashtags

A hashtag is used to mark keywords so that content related to that keyword can be easily found. A hashtag uses the pound or hash sign "#" for marking or highlighting a keyword or any topic on social media. It is a metadata tag used for tagging or cross-referencing content as per themes or topics across social media.

Hashtags were first used on Twitter (now X) after which they gained huge popularity and were then used across other social media platforms like Facebook and Instagram. Hashtags not only provide the right context to interpret the tweets and

---

100. WebFX Team, "How Much Does Pinterest Advertising Cost?," WebFX, September 28, 2023, https://www.webfx.com/social-media/pricing/how-much-does-pinterest-advertising-cost/.

categorize tweets but also serve as a medium to promote tweets to reach more readers.[101] From the year 2009, Twitter (now X) started hyperlinking all hashtags in tweets and also introduced "Trending Topics" which displayed the most popular hashtags on its homepage.

Hashtags have grown to play a very important role in social media marketing as:

- They can be used to label and find niche social media content.

- They help in making content easily discoverable.

- Social media users can use hashtags to find content that is engaging and of their interest.

6.5.1 How can businesses use hashtags effectively?

Finding relevant and trending topics and keywords

You should identify the topics and hashtags that are trending on social media and take advantage of them to join the conversation and get more views for your posts or content. You can use various hashtag analytics and monitoring sites like Hashtagify, Hashtags.org, Trendsmap, etc. At the same time, you should also research the hashtags to ensure that there is no negative news associated with them and avoid using the wrong hashtags which may be damaging to your brand's reputation.

---

101. Sedhai, Surendra, and Sun, Aixin. "Hashtag recommendation for hyperlinked tweets."SIGIR '14: Proceedings of the International ACM SIGIR Conference on Research and Development in Information Retrieval. (July, 2014):831-834. https://www.researchgate.net/publication/266658631_Hashtag_recommendation_for_hyperlinked_tweets

Knowing the social media platform

Each social media platform has different requirements and using too many hashtags may result in reduced engagement. The ideal number of hashtags for different social media platforms is:

- **1-2** hashtags on **Facebook**.

- **1-3** hashtags on **LinkedIn.** If it exceeds 5, the post could be marked as spam.

- **1-2** hashtags per tweet on **Twitter.**

- **Up to 10** hashtags on Instagram though the **maximum limit is 30.**

- **1-2** hashtags on **Pinterest.**

Creating hashtags

You must create specific and unique hashtags that can engage the audience. They mustn't be too long and should also be easy to remember. The hashtag should fit the campaign and shouldn't be irrelevant.

Sharing hashtags

After creating unique, specific, relevant, and engaging hashtags, you can add them to posts, image or video descriptions, tweets, comments, etc. Examples: #ShareACoke by Coca-Cola, #LetsdoLunch by Dominos, #PutACanOnIt by Red Bull, etc.

| Figure 6.5 | Target Audience; Objectives and Pros and Cons of Various Social Media Platforms |

	Who is your audience?	How can you reach them?	What are your goals?			
	CHOOSING THE RIGHT SOCIAL MEDIA PLATFORM FOR YOUR BUSINESS					
	f	y	P	▶	in	◉
	1.3+ Billion users	600 Million users	70 Million users	1 Billion users	600 Million users	200 Million users
DEMOGRAPHICS	Ages 25-54 60% Female	Ages 18-29	Ages 18-35 80% Female	All ages	Ages 30-49	Ages 18-29
PURPOSE	Building Relationships	News & Articles; Conversation	"Scrapbooking"	Search "How To"	News & Articles; Conversation	Building Relationships Coversation
BEST FOR	Building Brand Loyalty	Public Relations	Lead Generations; Clothing, Art & Food Businesses	Brand Awareness Service industry	Business Development: B2B Businesses	Lead Generation Retail, Art, Food, Entertainment, & Beauty Businesses
DOWNSIDE	Limited Reach	140 characters or less	Images only: Very specific demographic	Resource intensive	Limited interactions	Images only

Source: https://2.bp.blogspot.com/-G2IYO-pkvJE/WbYUksntdwI/
AAAAAAAAEUs/9PO7-jvV4NonVvx1l3sdqnqmNzvE1tDggCLcBGAs/s1600/mm2.png

6.5.2 Incorrect Use of Hashtags and How to Avoid Them

It is often observed that many businesses make mistakes while using hashtags. Using poor hashtags or using hashtags incorrectly may defeat their purpose and make the marketing effort to be ineffective. Therefore, you should avoid the following mistakes while using hashtags:

1. **Using hashtags that are "too" popular or generic**
    One common mistake businesses commit while using hashtags is using ones that are too popular or generic. Firstly, though popular hashtags may get you likes, they may not necessarily be from people who are actually interested in the brand. Secondly, the popular and generic hashtags are used so frequently that your post may get lost

in the crowd, as the list keeps getting updated rapidly, at lightning speed.

Hence, it is important to research the target audience and use hashtags that are specific to the target audience, product category, or industry. Using smaller and specifically targeted hashtags will not only help in reaching the target audience but also help your post reach the top posts in the section of hashtags you are using.

2. **Not researching hashtags before using them**
    Another mistake businesses make is not conducting proper research on hashtags. Sometimes, a hashtag may bring up inappropriate, malicious, or completely irrelevant images or posts which may negatively affect the brand. Hence you must enter the hashtag on Instagram or X search and check what kind of images or content pops up. There are many tools available to research hashtags such as TagsFinder, Ritetag, Metahashtags, Keyhole, hashtags.org, and many more which you can use.

3. **Ignoring capitalization when the hashtag contains more than one word**
    Sometimes, businesses may use multiple words in a hashtag. In this case, capitalizing each word makes the hashtag easy to read for the audience. For example, #lovelikeamother or #restandrelaxallday are not as easy to read as #LoveLikeAMother and #RestAndRelaxAllDay. Capitalizing each word in the hashtag also makes the hashtag more accessible as a screen reader will read each capitalized word separately rather than stringing them into one word.

4. **Using the same hashtags every day**

   If you use the same hashtags every day, they may lose relevance. Moreover, using the exact same set of hashtags with each post carries the risk of your account being treated as spam, and hence, it may no longer show up in the hashtag search results.

   To avoid this, you must create a repository of 50-60 hashtags which can easily be rotated on every post. This will help you to avoid the post being considered as spam.

5. **Using too many hashtags**

   Some businesses use too many hashtags in a post. When too many hashtags are used, readers may lose interest in reading so many of them and may ignore the post altogether. Too many hashtags may also make the post appear as spam. Hence, you must use a decent number of hashtags, say 2-4 per post, which will do the required job.

6. **Not using hashtags at all**

   Hashtags help the brand gain exposure, appear in the top section of trending posts, and reach a larger audience. For businesses that are looking to build their brand on social media, and gain engagement, even a little exposure can go a long way, and hashtags help brands gain that exposure. Used effectively and strategically, hashtags can help brands reach the target audience effectively and achieve growth. Hence you must not avoid using them and must jump onto the hashtag bandwagon to make your social media marketing efforts more effective.

Quiz

1. **X has around 238 million global _____.**

    a. registered users

    b. Monetizable Daily Active Users

    c. Monetizable Monthly Active Users

    d. other informational websites

2. **CTR stands for _____.**

    a. Current Transaction Rates

    b. Clicks Transaction Rates

    c. Current Tweet Rate

    d. Click-Through Rates

3. **Sponsored content, sponsored messaging, dynamic ads, and text ads are types of LinkedIn ads.**

    a. True

    b. False

4. **There are 3 kinds of Twitter ads:**

    a. Promoted ads, Follower ads, and Trend Takeover

    b. Image ads, Collection ads, and Carousel ads

    c. Text ads, Dynamic ads, and Promoted ads

    d. Sponsored messaging, Promoted ads, and Trend Takeover

5. **LinkedIn operates on a bidding model, like the other social media platforms.**

   a. True

   b. False

6. **YouTube is considered a strong tool for marketers because-**

   a. It is the second most popular social media platform.

   b. YouTube can improve the SEO for a brand.

   c. It has videos which are an effective medium as compared to text or images.

   d. All of the above

7. **A very large percentage of all small businesses in the US use YouTube, though producing videos is a tedious activity and is also expensive for small businesses.**

   a. True

   b. False

8. **The cost of YouTube ads depends on the number of**
   _____.

   a. views

   b. bids

   c. minutes

   d. None of the above

9. Hashtags were first used on_____.

    a. Facebook

    b. Instagram

    c. X

    d. LinkedIn

10._____are also known as content creators.

    a. YouTubers

    b. Social media analysts

    c. Influencers

    d. None of the above

Answers	1 − b	2 − d	3 − a	4 − a	5 − a
	6 − d	7 − b	8 − a	9 − c	10 − c

Chapter Summary

◆ With around 238 million global Monetizable Daily Active Users (mDAU), X has a large reach.

◆ Businesses that want to market on X must conduct an audit, research the audience, set marketing objectives, create a branded and customized profile, and then carry out their marketing activities.

◆ After Elon Musk's takeover, Twitter has been rebranded to "X" and Tweets are now called "posts".

◆ Since its takeover, X has lost both users and advertisers and it remains to be seen where it goes from here.

◆ There are 3 types of X ads: Promoted ads, Follower ads, and Trend Takeover.

◆ The cost of promoted tweets ranges from $0.50 to $2.00 for each action. Promoted accounts, on the other hand, cost between $2 and $4 per follower. Promoted trends are the most expensive of the three and they cost $200,000 per day.

◆ LinkedIn is considered a significant tool in B2B Marketing.

◆ LinkedIn, boasting a registered user base exceeding 830 million and over 310 million active daily users, including 180 million senior-level executives, offers businesses access to a target audience comprised of key decision-makers.

◆ LinkedIn marketing is done in two ways: Starting a free Company LinkedIn page and using LinkedIn ads.

◆ There are many types of LinkedIn ads like sponsored content, sponsored messaging, dynamic ads, and text ads.

◆ The CPC i.e., Cost Per Click for LinkedIn ads starts at a minimum of $2 but the average CPC is around $5.26 per click and the CPM is around $6.59 per 1000 impressions.

◆ Over 68% of active internet users have said that watching YouTube videos has helped them make a purchase decision.

◆ Businesses can do YouTube marketing by creating original videos, running video ads, and/or partnering with influencers.

◆ The cost of YouTube ads depends on the number of views. Each view costs between $0.10 to $0.30, depending on the target keywords and industry. The average cost to reach 100,000 viewers is approximately $2000.

◆ Studies have shown that over 80% of Pinterest Users (Pinners) have made a purchase based on brand content they saw on Pinterest.

◆ Pinterest ads have 4 formats: standard ads, video Ads, carousel ads, and collection ads.

◆ The cost of Pinterest ads is as follows: Cost Per Click (CPC) is between $0.10 - $1.50, Cost Per Thousand impressions (CPM) falls between $2.00 - $5.00, and Cost Per Conversion is between $6.00 - $10.00.

◆ A hashtag is used to mark keywords so that content related to that keyword can be easily found. A hashtag is defined as using the pound or hash (#) sign to mark or highlight a keyword or any topic on social media.

◆ Businesses must avoid the incorrect use of hashtags and use them effectively to market their products in a better way to reach their target audience more effectively and build strong brands on social media.

◆ Businesses should use hashtags effectively by finding relevant topics and keywords, researching social media platforms, and creating and sharing unique, specific, relevant, and engaging hashtags.

Chapter **7**

Metrics of Social Media Marketing

A very important part of a social media marketing strategy is evaluating the effectiveness of the social media activities undertaken by any business. For this evaluation, you can use several metrics. This chapter explains the process of evaluating a social media marketing program and discusses the major social media metrics, their importance, usage, and their calculation methods. After reading this chapter, you will get a clear understanding of how to evaluate/measure the effectiveness of your social media activities/program.

The key learning objectives should include the reader's understanding of the following:

- What is meant by social media metrics?

- What is the process of evaluating a social media marketing program?

- What are the major social media marketing metrics?

- How are they calculated?

- What is their importance and why are they used?

Social media metrics are the data used to assess the impact of social media activity on marketing campaigns and a company's revenue[102] . These metrics help to assess how well you are accomplishing your goals in the social space and provide insights for modifying your campaign, if required .

Social media metrics show you how well your social media strategy is performing. They help you understand how many people have seen your content, how much money you have spent on it, and how much you have earned from it. So, in simple words, social media metrics are a part of evaluating the social media program of any business. You need to know whether your social media strategies are working, whether your social media plan is effective, and what needs to be changed to increase the effectiveness. Social media metrics, thus, help in understanding the overall impact of your social media presence by understanding the social media profile and brand health.

Social media metrics depend on the goals you have set for your social media marketing. For example, if you have published ads on social media to increase website traffic and conversions, you need to measure these metrics, i.e. the traffic and conversion rate using various analytics.

Before delving more into social media metrics, let us take a

---

102. "Social Media Metrics," BrightEdge, n.d., https://www.brightedge.com/glossary/social-media-metrics.

look at the process of evaluation of social media marketing carried out by a business. Any plan or strategy is successful only if it achieves results or fulfills its objectives. To understand whether your social media marketing campaign is successful or not, you need to evaluate it by following the process as described below:

7.1 Process of Evaluation of a Social Media Marketing Program

Figure 7.1 Evaluating a social media marketing program

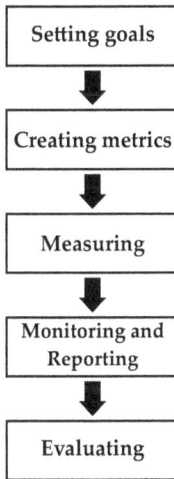

```
        ┌─────────────────┐
        │  Setting goals  │
        └────────┬────────┘
                 ▼
        ┌─────────────────┐
        │ Creating metrics│
        └────────┬────────┘
                 ▼
        ┌─────────────────┐
        │    Measuring    │
        └────────┬────────┘
                 ▼
        ┌─────────────────┐
        │ Monitoring and  │
        │    Reporting    │
        └────────┬────────┘
                 ▼
        ┌─────────────────┐
        │   Evaluating    │
        └─────────────────┘
```

1. Setting goals

The first step in the evaluation of social media marketing is to create a list of the goals or objectives of the social media marketing campaigns. Based on the kind of content and target audience, you can decide which social media platforms to use and what to achieve through each of them. For example, if a company ABC manufactures mobile phones, and wants to educate customers about the features of their new handset and demonstrate them, they may decide to create an unboxing video demonstrating the camera and video quality, screen refresh rate, and other functions. To achieve this goal, they may decide to use YouTube to share this detailed video.

2. Creating Metrics

The next step in the evaluation process is to match the goals to actual metrics and behaviors that can be measured. You can measure various behaviors like the number of re-tweets, comments, shares, replies, and so on. For example, if you want to measure website traffic generated through social media, you can check URL clicks, shares, and conversions. You can check whether people are visiting the website from the social media page or an ad and also track their activity once they visit your brand's website. You can check engagement by checking metrics related to reposts, replies, comments, re-tweets, and the number of interactions.

3. Measuring

Once you have identified the metrics you need to concentrate on, you should find the tools that can capture these metrics so that you can start measuring them. While many social media platforms themselves provide some form of analytics, you may need to use third-party tools. It is easy to identify which tools to use, as a quick Google search will provide answers. Social media analytics tools are effective as they work in real-time making it easier to evaluate the data. So, you can set up the tracking before the social media marketing campaign begins. Few examples of such tools include Google Analytics, Keyhole, Audiense, Social Pilot, Mention, Hootsuite, Sprout Social, etc.

For example, on Twitter, it is very difficult and expensive to access tweets that are more than a few days old. It is much easier, more cost-effective, and more reliable to collect and archive tweets in real-time. Hence, you should set up tracking before their social media marketing campaigns begin.

4. Monitoring and Reporting

After measuring the data, the next step is to create reports containing the results. It is a good idea to use the preliminary findings to set a benchmark that can be used for future measurements. These early figures can also be shared with stakeholders. You should check whether what you had expected is similar to what you have achieved. If your achievement falls short of your expected numbers, you should try to identify the reasons for it. You should also compare these with industry numbers, like those of your competitors, or related products and services, which will give you an idea of whether your achieved numbers are in line with industry numbers. This is where social media analytics proves extremely beneficial, as it helps in easily running reports about competitors to understand how they're performing.

You can also create a schedule for regular reporting. You can opt for daily, weekly, fortnightly, monthly, or quarterly reports based on your requirements. It is extremely beneficial for you to collect these metrics as, over time, you will have created a repository of data that you can use to compare with your present and future data.

5. Evaluating

The fifth and last step is to evaluate the measurement program carefully to identify whether anything is missed, how the metrics are performing, whether there's anything that isn't needed or useful, etc. You should conduct a careful review of your program to find out what changes can be made and how you can improve. By evaluating the social media marketing campaigns on various platforms, you will learn what audiences liked or found interesting, what engaged them more, and whether the campaign had the expected impact. These revelations can be used in the next campaign to make it more effective.

7.2 Parameters to Measure the Impact of Social Media Marketing (Social Media Marketing Metrics)

There are many metrics that you can use to measure the impact of a social media marketing campaign. Let us look at some of the major social media marketing metrics:

1. Engagement

As we have seen in previous chapters, one of the differentiating factors between traditional and social media is customer or audience engagement. Hence businesses that want to engage their customers use social media to achieve it. Some of the basic social media metrics that are needed to understand engagement are:

- Likes

- Comments

- Shares

- Retweets

- Clicks

These metrics show how engaging and interactive your social media content is. They enhance your business' and brand's credibility. Engagement can be measured in two ways:

- By looking separately at the exact number of likes, comments, retweets, and shares. This data can also be used to count the average or median for each type of engagement.

- By calculating the engagement rate, which shows the level of engagement with the published content. There are various tools available for calculating the engagement rate.

Social media engagement is defined as the total number of likes, comments, shares, and general interactions that a piece of content or social media account receives relative to the size of the audience[103]. Having a large following isn't useful if your audience isn't regularly interacting with your content.

To measure the overall engagement rate of a social media account, you can use the following formula:

$$\text{Engagement Rate} = \frac{\text{Number of Engagements}}{\text{Number of Followers}} \times 100$$

---

103. Jan Tegze, "Why Your LinkedIn Posts Matter More than You Think," Jan Tegze, February 8, 2023, https://jantegze.com/blog/why-your-linkedin-posts-matter-more-than-you-think/.

2. Reach & Impressions

Reach is defined as the number of people who see a business' content. You must monitor the average reach of your content, and also the reach of your individual posts, stories, or videos.

A valuable subset of this metric is to look at what percentage of your reach is made up of followers vs. non-followers. If your content reaches a lot of non-followers, it means that it's being shared or doing well in the algorithms, or both. On YouTube, the total number of video views can be considered as the reach. The number of views, mentions, number of subscribers, followers, and fans are calculated to understand the reach of the given social media platform.

Impressions are the number of times people saw your content.[104] It is also known as frequency and can be higher than reach because the same user might view the content more than once. It is good to have a high level of impressions compared to reach as it indicates that people are looking at a post multiple times. However, all social media platforms measure impressions differently. For example, on Facebook, every time a user sees a paid ad on screen, it is considered an impression; whereas on Twitter, each time a user sees a tweet is considered an impression. On Instagram each time a user views a piece of content such as an ad, story, reel, etc., it is counted as an impression.

3. Social Share of Voice (SSoV)

The share of voice, known as social share of voice for social media, measures how many people are talking about a business' brand on all social channels. It finds all the total mentions that a

---

104. Christina Newberry, "17 Social Media Metrics You Need to Track in 2023 [BENCHMARKS]," Social Media Marketing & Management Dashboard, August 2, 2023, https://blog.hootsuite.com/social-media-metrics/.

brand has received. A large number of mentions indicate good brand awareness. It indicates that your brand is getting visible on social media and helps you updates and improve your social media strategy. Social share of voice is calculated by measuring the business' product/brand mentions across all its social networks. Social media analytics tools can be used to calculate this number. This can also be compared with competitors to find the industry share of voice for a particular business in comparison with its competitors.

For example, if a business like McDonald's has found that in a given period it has been mentioned directly and indirectly 200 times and its competitors like Burger King, Wendy's, Taco Bell, and KFC have 800 mentions. So the total industry mentions are 1000(Competitors' 800 + McDonald's = 1000.) So, McDonald's Social Share of Voice will be calculated as:

200/1000*100 i.e. 20%. So, their SSoV will be 20%.

4. Response Rate and Time

Studies have shown that over 70% of respondents engage with the brands that they follow on social media. They may make inquiries, leave reviews, and respond to advertisements. It is important for businesses to respond to as many social media mentions as possible. For tracking this, they can check their customer response rate. To calculate the customer response rate, one must divide the number of responses given to their followers/ customers by the number of people who engaged with the brand and multiply it by 100.

For example, if you measured a month of engagement, and found that the number of customers who engaged with your brand was 100, and the business responded to 75 customers, your customer response rate would be 75%.

Response time is the average time taken by a business to respond to a customer on its social media page. Studies have shown that most customers expect responses within 24 hours, while few expect responses within an hour. If you are quick to respond, it results in increased brand loyalty.

5. Influencer Campaign Metrics

Influence scores are used to measure how influential a particular person or brand is on a given social media channel. Influencer marketing is a growing phenomenon used by marketers on social media. Most social media sites are flooded with influencers. Influencers can be leveraged by business to improve their sales. Influencers endorse your product or service with social credibility, act as brand ambassadors on digital media and create and spread a good word about the brand. Choosing the right influencer, who has a good number of followers is important for achieving a successful social media marketing campaign.

One of the basic metrics for tracking influencer marketing campaigns is the return on investment (ROI). ROI is the revenue or profit generated from an influencer campaign divided by the cost.[105]

A social media monitoring tool checks the talk around your brand or your industry niche (depending on your social media monitoring project) and prepares a list of the most influential profiles already talking about your brand. Businesses must check the engagement rate, post frequency, number of followers, comments/likes ratio, follower growth, cost per post, branded

---

105. Dave Lavinsky. "Influencer Marketing Metrics You Should Be Tracking - Supermetrics," November 17, 2021. https://supermetrics.com/blog/influencer-marketing-metrics.

posts, and quality score of influencers before using them in their marketing campaign.

An influencer campaign is one of the most effective campaigns on social media. Influencer marketing is growing rapidly and has crossed $10 billion globally in 2021.[106]

6. Audience Growth Rate

Just having an audience isn't enough. It is important to add new followers and new visitors to the business' social media pages and increase the audience size. To measure the audience growth rate, the business must first select a reporting period. Then, they must calculate the new followers that have joined during that particular period. After that, they need to divide the new followers by the total followers and multiply that figure by 100.

For example, your Twitter account has 10,000 followers at a given point in time and you gain 2000 new followers in a given period. The audience growth rate for the particular period will be calculated as 2000 divided by 10000 multiplied by 100 i.e. 20%.

7. Social Media Conversion Rate

A conversion happens when a user does what the business intended him/her to do. In other words, social media conversion means that a user completes an action with the business that originated from social media. The social media conversion rate of a business consists of the number of visitors to its website that take a desired action. These actions could include signing up for the

---

106. Grand View Research. "Influencer Marketing Platform Market Size, Share & Trends Analysis Report By Application, By Organization Size, By End-Use, By Region, And Segment Forecasts, 2022 - 2030," n.d. https://www.grandviewresearch.com/industry-analysis/influencer-marketing-platform-market.

business' newsletter, downloading the business' eBook, or clicking "Play" on their podcast. Conversion rates show how relevant your content is to your audience.

The conversion rate is calculated by dividing your number of conversions from social media traffic by the number of website visitors. A high conversion rate indicates a high level of interest and engagement with a brand's content on social media platforms. Conversions may include any of the following actions:

- aking a purchase
- Signing up for the company's newsletter
- Filling out a form
- Subscribing to a blog
- Calling the business
- Using their online chat
- Starting a product trial
- Downloading the app or e-book
- Visiting the company website
- Playing the company's podcast

8. ROI

This is a major and crucial metric that all businesses aim to achieve from their social media marketing campaigns. ROI (return on investment) is the return a company receives from its social media activities and expenses.

Social media ROI is a measure of all social media actions that create value, divided by the investment made to achieve those actions.[107] Businesses need to know how much tangible returns they have received for the time, effort, and money that they have put in. When it comes to social media, businesses want to know if the time, effort, and money they have spent on social media is converting into sales, customers, or brand awareness. Depending on the company and industry, the return on investment can vary largely. ROI is calculated in the following manner:

$$\text{Social media ROI } \% = \frac{\text{Profit}}{\text{Investment}} \times 100$$

Where **Profit** is the money earned from the business' social media marketing efforts and **Investment** is the total cost incurred on the social media marketing efforts of the business.

Most marketers consider the following metrics as important markers to measure their social media ROI:

- Engagement (likes/comments/clicks/tweets/shares)
- Traffic to their website
- Views
- Sales i.e. revenue generated
- Reach (views/mentions/subscribers/followers etc.)

9. Traffic to Brand's Website

Many companies consider traffic to their website a high-priority metric. It is known as social traffic. It refers to traffic coming to a website or a mobile app, from social media

---

107. Laura Wong, "How to Prove (and Improve!) Your Social Media ROI," Social Media Marketing & Management Dashboard, September 21, 2023, https://blog.hootsuite.com/measure-social-media-roi-business/.

platforms.[108] For example, if a user clicks on a promotional post on Facebook which takes them to your business' website, this will be recorded in your business analytics reports as social traffic. Traffic to the brand's website increases conversions, improves brand awareness, and gives users more information about the products. Hence, businesses aim to generate traffic to their website through their social media marketing campaigns.

This social traffic may be paid or organic. To find how much traffic is generated, you must aim to find how many of the page views are coming directly from social media. Web traffic tools such as Google Analytics are used for measuring how much of a business' traffic comes from social media.

10. Audience Insights

The seventh crucial metric is the audience growth rate. But it is not just the growth rate that is important. You must also focus on your existing audience. How much do you know about your current audience?

The key audience demographics that you must consider include:

- Age

- Gender

- Income level

- Education

- Geographic location

- Occupation/Designation

---

108. SocialBee, "Traffic Meaning | Social Media Marketing Definitions - SocialBee," October 4, 2022, https://socialbee.com/glossary/traffic/.

- Marital status

- Number of people in the household

Social media platforms such as Instagram and Facebook provide you with audience insights by providing aggregated information about user demographics of people connected to your page(s). Meaningful insights into demographics, people's likes, dislikes, habits, interests, hobbies, and lifestyles are provided which help you zero in on your target audience, understand what they need, and design marketing programs accordingly.

11. Net Promoter Score (NPS)

The Net Promoter Score (NPS) is one of the important metrics that you need to track. Studies have shown that over 80% of people trust the recommendations made by their friends and family more than they trust advertising.[109] NPS helps to measure customers that are loyal to the brand. It is a tool used to determine and measure if your customers will refer you to new people.[110] NPS is considered an ideal way to find out whether the business' recommendation efforts are successful.

NPS serves as a customer satisfaction benchmark that measures the overall sentiment felt by a new customer towards the brand. To find the Net Promoter Score, businesses ask customers how likely they are to recommend them to a friend. Companies use three categories for tracking NPS. Customers are asked to rate the business from 1-10. Scorers that answer 9-10 are called "Promoters.", scorers that answer 7-8 are called "Passives", and

---

109. Sprout Social, "What Is Net Promoter Score (NPS)? | Sprout Social," September 28, 2023, https://sproutsocial.com/glossary/net-promoter-score/.

110. Influencer Marketing Hub, "What Is Net Promoter Score (NPS)?," January 27, 2022, https://influencermarketinghub.com/glossary/net-promoter-score-nps/.

"Detractors" are those that answer 0-6. For calculating NPS, one must subtract "Detractors" from "Promoters" and divide that by the total number of respondents. Then, multiply that number by 100. For example, if a company has 100 "Promoters" and 20 "Detractors" from a survey of 150 respondents, their NPS would be calculated as: (100-20)/150 x 100 i.e. 53.33%.

Did you know?

There are hundreds of metrics to measure social media marketing. Though the major ones have been discussed in this chapter, there are many others such as impressions, buzz, virality rate, amplification rate, video completion rate, social sentiment, CSAT (Customer Satisfaction Score), friends, followers, downloads and uploads, ratings, social bookmarks, frequency of interactions per customer, and many more.

Quiz

1. _____is the data used to assess the impact of social media activity on marketing campaigns and a company's revenue.

   a. Social media platforms

   b. Social media analytics

   c. Social media metrics

   d. Social media strategies

2. _____ is the second step in the process of evaluation of the social media marketing program.

   a. Setting goals

   b. Measuring

   c. Creating Metrics

   d. Monitoring and Reporting

3. The fifth and last step is to evaluate the social media marketing program carefully to identify whether anything is missed and how the metrics are performing.

   a. True

   b. False

4. _____is the total number of likes, comments, shares, and general interactions a piece of content or social media account receives relative to the size of the audience.

   a. Social media engagement

   b. Social media metrics

   c. Reach

   d. Conversions

5. The number of views, mentions, subscribers, followers, and fans are calculated to understand the _____of the given social media platform.

   a. impressions

   b. reach

   c. engagement

   d. response

6. The _____ for social media measures how many people are talking about a business's brand on all social channels.

   a. social share of voice

   b. impressions

   c. engagement

   d. reach

7. Impressions are also known as frequency and can be higher than reach because the same user might look at the content more than once.

   a. True

   b. False

8. Response time is the average time taken by a business to find its target customers on various social media pages.

   a. True

   b. False

9. A _____ checks the talk around your brand or your industry niche and prepares a list of the most influential profiles already talking about your brand.

   a. influencer marketing tool

   b. social media monitoring tool

   c. profile monitoring tool

   d. None of the above

10. To measure the audience growth rate, the business must first select a_____.

   a. social media strategy

   b. target follower rate

   c. market segment

   d. reporting period

Answers	1 − c	2 − c	3 − a	4 − a	5 − b
	6 − a	7 − a	8 − b	9 − b	10 − d

Chapter Summary

◆ Social media metrics show you how well your social media strategy is performing. They help you understand how many people have seen your content, how much money you have spent on it, and how much you have earned from it.

◆ Social media metrics depend on the goals set by the business for its social media marketing. For example, if you have published ads on social media with the goal of increasing website traffic and conversions, you will need to measure these metrics, that is, the traffic and conversion rate using various analytics.

◆ The process of evaluation of a social media marketing program includes setting goals, creating metrics, measuring, monitoring, reporting, and finally evaluating the program.

◆ Social media engagement includes the number of likes, comments, shares, and general interactions received by a piece of content or social media account relative to the size of the audience.

◆ Reach is the number of people who have seen a business' content whereas impressions are the number of times people saw the content.

◆ The share of voice, known as social share of voice for social media, measures how many people are talking about a business' brand on all social channels

◆ Response time is the average time taken by a business to respond to a customer on its social media page.

◆ Influence scores are used to measure how influential a particular person or brand is on a given social media channel. Influencer marketing is a growing phenomenon used by marketers on social media.

◆ Influencers endorse your product or service with social credibility. An influencer acts as a brand ambassador on digital media and creates and spreads a good word about the brand.

◆ The social media conversion rate of a business consists of the number of visitors to its website that take a desired action. These actions could include signing up for a newsletter, downloading an eBook, or clicking "Play" on a podcast.

◆ ROI is the return a company receives from its social media activities and expenses.

◆ Many companies consider traffic to their website a high-priority metric. Social traffic refers to incoming traffic to a website or mobile app from social media platforms.

◆ Social media platforms such as Instagram and Facebook provide businesses with meaningful insights into demographics, people's likes, dislikes, habits, interests, hobbies, and lifestyles which help businesses zero in on their target audience, understand what they need, and design marketing programs accordingly.

◆ Net Promoter Score (NPS) is a tool used to determine and measure if your customers will refer you to new people. It is considered an ideal way to find out whether the business's recommendation efforts are successful.

Chapter **8**

Ethics in Social Media Marketing

Many times, we focus on profits and growth, and ignore an important aspect of marketing – ethics. When you engage in social media marketing, you engage with the public, including your customers. As a part of the society, it is your ethical and moral responsibility to avoid unethical practices. In the long run, being ethical will prove beneficial to you as you earn people's trust, a positive brand image, and better goodwill. This chapter highlights certain ethical issues in social media marketing and further discusses the fundamental ethics and best practices you can follow while implementing your social media marketing campaign.

The key learning objectives should include the reader's understanding of the following:

- What are ethics?

- What are social media marketing ethics?

- Are ethics really needed in social media marketing?

- What ethical issues are seen in social media marketing?

- What are the fundamental ethics of social media marketing?

- Which are the best ethical practices in social media marketing that companies should follow?

We are constantly evolving into a technologically advanced world and as we continue to technologically develop, there are many unprecedented ethical and moral dilemmas that we have to face. Today, social media has blurred the lines between real life and technology. As with other marketing avenues, social media marketing hasn't been immune to unethical practices.

Marketing ethics focus on principles and standards that define acceptable marketing conduct but we must emphasize that today, marketing ethics go beyond legal, regulatory, and marketing issues which help build long-term marketing relationships.[111] Thus, using ethics in marketing implies using the right conduct, i.e. being fair, unbiased, honest, transparent, and moral in each aspect of marketing like decision making, strategies, behavior, and practice in the organization.

111. Dincer Caner, and Dinçer Banu. "An Overview and Analysis of Marketing Ethics." International Journal of Academic Research in Business & Social Sciences 4, no. 11 (November 25, 2014): 151-158. http://dx.doi.org/10.6007/IJARBSS/v4-i11/1290

Ethics help improve a company's market position against its immediate competitors.[112]

Social media marketing is an unprecedented blend of the personal and the professional which provides businesses with extremely intimate consumer data. Recently, we have seen privacy concerns surrounding Facebook, Twitter, and other sites in the news. This has raised various questions about the digital world, data, bias, transparency, and privacy. Social media marketers use the data collected by various social media sites to create marketing strategies and target their prospective customers but they need to ensure that they are doing this ethically.

A company that does not employ ethical practices may be perceived negatively, which may lead to loss of trust and business, dissatisfaction among customers, negative publicity, and even lead to legal actions.

Being ethical means being right, fair, just, moral, principled, responsible, honorable, conscientious, behaving with integrity, and respecting others' rights and choices. A company that works in the public domain, especially when it markets its products on social media, has to make its social media content accessible to everyone. You must ask yourselves various questions before posting any content:

- Are we being honest?
- Can this content be considered hateful?

---

112. V.S. Dhole. "Ethics in Marketing." Vidyabharati International Interdisciplinary Research Journal 9(2). (December 2019): 155-157. https://www.researchgate.net/profile/Vikas-Dole-3/publication/354651377_ETHICS_IN_MARKETING/links/6144435ad5f4292c01fe8ae3/ETHICS-IN-MARKETING.pdf

- Is this content true and complete or are we hiding certain facts?

- Are we misrepresenting any information?

- Are we being fair or are we being biased?

- Are we collecting customer data without permission?

- Are we giving customers the choice to say no, to unsubscribe, and to protect their privacy and other rights?

- Are we being malicious?

- Are we misleading the audience?

- Are we securing the customer/audience data we have collected with their permission?

- Are we verifying the content before posting?

Once all these questions are answered, you must look into ethical areas where you are falling short, or if there is any scope for improvement.

Figure 8.1 Ethics/Ethical values

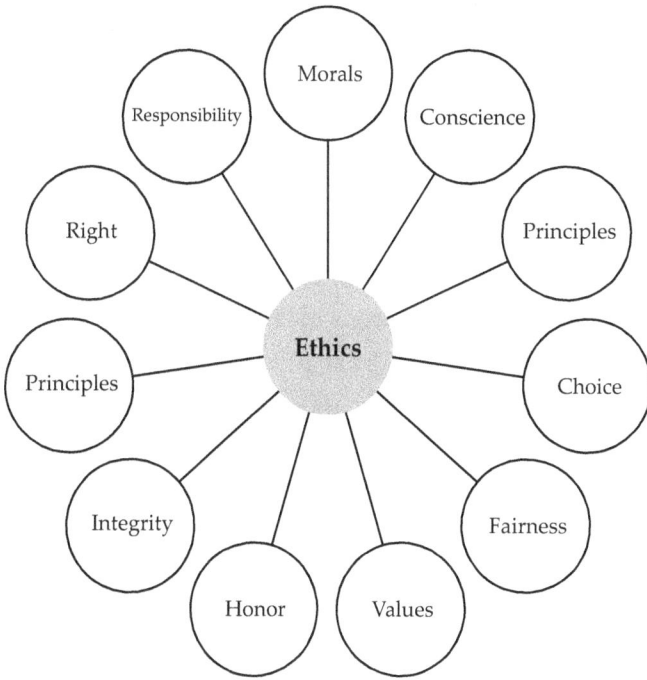

8.1 Ethical Issues in Social Media Marketing

When we talk about ethics, we need to understand what can be considered unethical in any functional area. It might be noted that ethics are considered a moral philosophy. They include moral values and the distinction between what is right and what is wrong. Businesses in their lifetime are faced with several ethical dilemmas. Choosing the right path may often conflict with your objectives of earning profits or generating revenue. You need to have a value-oriented framework. While unethical practices may succeed in the short run, in the long run, consumers may end up distrusting the brand, resulting in a negative brand image.

Therefore, it is always better for you to be ethical, to avoid facing huge problems in the long run. There are many ways in which social media marketing can be unethical. Some of the major ethical issues are:

1. Consumer Privacy

The reason for the success of social media marketing among businesses is its ability to target users based on their demographics. There are various cookies and online trackers that collect information about users such as their place of residence, their online buying habits, their age, political opinions, religious beliefs, interests, and so on. While this is beneficial for companies who can use this data to target their prospective customers and design marketing programs that would be more effective, it may pose the question of breach of privacy. Was the consumer's consent taken before accessing his personal data? Was he made aware of the company's privacy policy? Does he wish to share his intimate data? These are some questions that are raised these days. Consumers today are aware that their data is being used by companies, but they expect this data to be used ethically. This means that it shouldn't be used for any other purpose than the one mentioned in the privacy policy or explicitly informed to consumers. Also, consumer data should not be collected without their knowledge or by misleading them. It must be noted that the concept of privacy, its meaning, framework, and importance varies across different cultures, countries, regions, domains, and organizations, and hence, the privacy expectations from customers, the general public, employees, and other stakeholders may differ accordingly. What may be considered normal practice in one country, like in the US, may be looked upon as a gross invasion of privacy in another country like China. Privacy regulations, too, differ from country to country. For example, privacy is viewed very differently in North Korea as compared to South Korea. In North Korea, citizens and visitors aren't allowed to speak ill of the country or its leaders. Doing so can lead to punishment. Conversations and cell phone activity are monitored by the authorities. So, businesses, including social media platforms, must understand the privacy considerations in the countries and regions where they operate.

2. Lack of Transparency

One trend very commonly seen these days is placing advertising content in such a way that it seems to be information or facts rather than what it actually is: an advertisement. Many influencers are paid to review products. The ethical thing to do here is to inform customers that it is a sponsored review. The more transparent and open the company is, the more trust the audience will have in them. For example, let's consider a situation. A restaurant gives a popular food blogger a free meal, hoping for a social media review. Though the restaurant might go the extra mile for the influencer, it's important for them to be honest. Telling followers about the free meal keeps things real and helps followers judge the experience. If followers visit and find issues, the influencer's honesty about the free meal explains things and keeps trust intact. Open communication, like being clear about the free meal, builds trust between the influencer, followers, and the restaurant.

3. Lack of data security

Cybercrime is extremely prevalent in the digital world. When customers access a social media page or site, their data is stored on the company's servers. Sometimes, personal, private, and intimate information such as name, age, address, gender, purchasing habits, browsing history, etc. may be accessed and saved for analysis on the servers. If the company doesn't take adequate care to secure its servers, this data becomes vulnerable to attacks from hackers. Hackers may steal the data by hacking the company's servers and using this data illegally. It could be used for further scams like phishing.[113] An ethical company must ensure that they are using various security measures to protect their consumers' intimate, personal data from hackers and third parties with ulterior motives.

4. Elimination of Bias

Everyone has an opinion and the right to express it. However, a company, being in the public domain, must maintain a balanced and fair online presence. You must refrain from making religious, political, racist, or controversial comments. An ethical company must steer away from expressing personal opinions related to religion, race, politics, caste, lifestyle choices, sexual orientation, or any other issues that may hurt people's sentiments. Insensitive comments can hurt and alienate many sections of your target audience. Even a single post or tweet can cost you several followers.

Example: In March 2017, McDonald's tweeted a political post from its official account that mocked the then-president of the US, comparing him to his predecessor and making personal comments on his physical appearance. This tweet was pinned to the top of their official page for a short while. After facing backlash, it was quickly deleted. However, it was able to generate over 1,000 likes and retweets. It garnered reactions from angry supporters

---

113. Phishing (pronounced: fishing) is an attack that attempts to steal your money, or your identity, by getting you to reveal personal information -- such as credit card numbers, bank information, or passwords -- on websites that pretend to be legitimate. *www.vibrantpublishers.com*

of the president who created the hashtag #BoycottMcDonalds. McDonald's then issued an apology and blamed some hacker for the tweet.[114]

5. Sharing Misleading or Unverified Information

You must always verify the information you are sharing online. You shouldn't make false claims, or share misleading or fake information which could affect your trustworthiness. If you post some false information, the audience may be able to prove it is false and this could result in backlash, negative comments, and loss of trust. Unverified claims such as "guaranteed weight loss in five days", "no side effects", "90% better than competitors", "kills 99.99% germs", or being "the #1 trusted brand" are very common. However, if they are backed up by research or authentic sources, they carry more weight and are perceived more positively by the audience. Hence, you need to check any information you're sharing, verify it from reliable sources, and refrain from sharing any information that is fake, false, unreliable, or unverified. This will increase your credibility in the audience's minds.

---

114. Jack Cieslak, "#Fail: 29 Of The Biggest Corporate Brand Social Media Flubs," CB Insights Research, September 28, 2017, https://www.cbinsights.com/research/corporate-social-media-fails/.

8.2 Fundamental Ethics of Social Media Marketing

Do Not Compromise on Privacy

Value the right to privacy of your audience. Do not violate any rules of privacy. Avoid spamming and give the audience the option to unsubscribe from promotional campaigns.

Be Honest

Always tell the truth about your company, your products or services and never lie or exaggerate about their performance, value, prices, customer service, returns process and so on.

Be Transparent

Don't try to hide any information. If the company endorses any person, movement, product, service or issue, they must reveal their reasons for doing so.

Secure Your Servers

Ensure that the consumers data is not compromised, leaked, used illegally or hacked by using cyber security to protect and secure data.

Do Not post malicious content about competitors

Ensure that you are practicing fair competition and not indulging in unfair practices. Malicious post about competitors can backfire and result in a competitive was which may harm the organization.

Check Before You Post/Tweet

Check whether the information you are sharing is authentic and true. Do no use unverified information and cite the sources wherever possible.

Avoid Bias

Do not take sides. Avoid political, religious, racial, ethnic, caste, sexual and cultural bias. Avoid hurting the sentiments of people.

Do Not Gather Data Unethically

Companies must not fool people into giving their data. The sudience's permission should be asked before collecting their data, especially sensitive, intimate, personal data such as age, address, income, purchasing information and history, browsing data, etc.

8.3 Best Practices for Ethical Social Media Marketing

Figure 8.2 **Best practices for social media marketing**

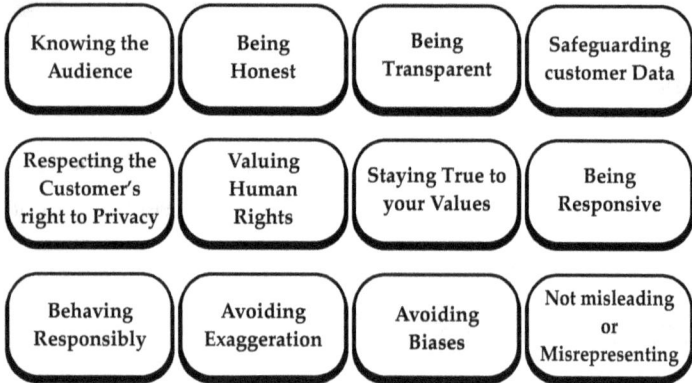

Knowing the Audience	Being Honest	Being Transparent	Safeguarding customer Data
Respecting the Customer's right to Privacy	Valuing Human Rights	Staying True to your Values	Being Responsive
Behaving Responsibly	Avoiding Exaggeration	Avoiding Biases	Not misleading or Misrepresenting

1. Knowing the Audience

Whenever you are posting anything on social media, you should know who it is being posted for.   and ensure that you are not hurting anyone's sentiments. You need to answer the following questions to gain an understanding of your audience:

- Who is your audience?

- Which social media sites do they access and how frequently?

- What is their occupation? Where do they work?

- Where do they live?

- What are their likes, dislikes, needs, wants, and preferences?

- How do they perceive your company?

- What are their expectations from your company, your products, and services?

2. Honest Communication

You need to be honest in all your social media communications.

Companies may tend to exaggerate figures to promote their own interests, such as inflating sales numbers, highlighting product benefits, and showcasing enticing offers. While a degree of embellishment may be acceptable, excessive stretching of the truth can lead to a detrimental perception. It is imperative to maintain honesty regarding the product, encompassing its features, ingredients, performance, uses, potential side effects, quality, and pricing. Addressing consumer inquiries with sincerity is equally crucial. For instance, if a customer lodges a complaint about late delivery on the company's social media page, the company should candidly acknowledge the mistake, offer a sincere apology, and propose a resolution. Embracing transparency in such instances fosters a positive atmosphere.

Figure 8.3 **Misleading advertisement images**

Source: YouTube   https://www.pinterest.com/pin/668714244672453493/

A customer may purchase a product based on the image he saw in the company's social media advertisement. If the product turns out to be drastically different from the one advertised, he is bound to be dissatisfied. Many times customers believe social media posts or advertisements that are misleading or misrepresentative and end up buying products that are significantly different from the ones advertised. Hence companies must be forthcoming to furnish real, true, and factual information, supported by proof, and not mislead the audience.

3. Transparency

Since a lot of information is easily accessible and available at one's fingertips, people expect brands to be more open about themselves. They may demand to know how the products are made, their country of origin, source of the materials used, type of materials used (for example: organic, eco-friendly), and anything else about the company, its brands, products, and/or services. According to Forbes, trust can be a powerful differentiator in defining and protecting a company's brand. This responsibility lies not solely with a security team, but across an organization, from sales to customer service, and top-down from executive leadership. Brands that earn consumers' trust are ultimately better equipped to focus on core revenue-generating activities that delight customers, grow brand affinity, and benefit their bottom line.[115]   While you don't need to share your trade secrets or confidential information, you should ensure that you are honest and transparent in your communication with your audience, followers, and customers.

115. Daniel Barber, "Why Brands That Opt For Transparency Are Winning," Forbes, December 29, 2020, https://www.forbes.com/sites/forbestechcouncil/2021/12/29/why-brands-that-opt-for-transparency-are-winning/?sh=162c36cf451e.

4. Safeguarding Customer Data and Respecting the Customers' Right to Privacy

Instagram was charged €405 million (over $400 million) under the European Union General Data Protection Regulation due to a privacy breach of children's data, including the spread of email addresses and phone numbers. This is the third time they have been fined under the Irish Data Protection Commission over security concerns.[116]

Facebook provides its business partners with tracking software they embed in apps, websites, and loyalty programs. Any business or group that needs to do digital advertising has little choice but to feed your activities into Facebook's vacuum: your grocer, politicians, and yes, even the paywall page for a newspaper's website. Behind the scenes, Facebook takes in this data and tries to match it up to your account. It is stored under your name in a part of your profile your friends can't see, but Facebook uses it to shape your experience online.

Among the 100 most popular smartphone apps, Facebook software can be found in 61 of them, according to app research firm Sensor Tower. Facebook also has trackers in about 25% of websites, according to privacy software maker Ghostery.[117]

116. Aneeka Chatterjee, "Instagram: Meta Hit with €405 Million over Children's Data Breach," BusinessLine, September 6, 2022, https://www.thehindubusinessline.com/info-tech/social-media/instagram-meta-hit-with-405-million-over-childrens-data-breach/article65856700.ece.

117. G1. Your privacy is the price of Facebook's Monopoly - The Washington Post, accessed December 20, 2023, https://www.washingtonpost.com/technology/2021/08/29/facebook-privacy-monopoly/.

With such news reports, customer data privacy and security issues have come under the limelight. Sometimes customer data is hacked and used illegally. In other cases, data is sold to other businesses. Phishing attacks, spam, and other scams have also been reported. Such unethical behavior can also impact their growth, as users may leave the sites due to privacy and data security concerns.

5. Valuing Human Rights

Another ethical issue to be considered in social media marketing is human rights and inclusivity in terms of language, imagery, etc. Human rights need to be respected and companies must not violate them.

According to Douwe Korff and Ian Brown[118], far from providing a free, unwatched space for social and political interaction, internet technologies can facilitate potentially comprehensive surveillance over online political action which is increasingly linked to offline surveillance of political activities, in particular through "social network analysis" and "profiling". This is happening not just in countries that are manifestly repressive but also in modern democracies, using compulsory suspicion-less mass communication data retention under the EU's Data Retention Directive. It has been found that such measures violate the fundamental rights and basic principles of the rule of law by national constitutional courts in several EU member states and by the European Data Protection.

Social media has been used to spread misinformation, incite violence, create political turmoil, and interfere in elections. It

---

118. Douwe Korff and Ian Brown. "Social Media and Human Rights." Commissioner for Human Rights, Strasbourg. February, 2012. https://rm.coe.int/16806da579

has been observed that a lot of the activism, organization, and civil society movements that everyone cares about, take place on platforms that were not designed for security. Moreover, governments and private surveillance companies that are hired by adversaries are employing digital tools and data collection to thwart human rights activists.[119] For example: Eli Lily & Co, a pharmaceutical giant in the US had to apologize after an impostor account tweeted that they were offering free insulin vaccines. This tweet resulted in a sharp fall in Eli Lily and Co's share prices. This tweet was the result of a fake account purchasing the 'blue-tick verified' label from Twitter. This incident, along with many similar ones that followed, forced Twitter to stop offering this premium service that was available to anyone who paid a certain fee.

Hence, there is a grave need for social media companies to respect human rights and come up with measures to put a stop to such practices.

6. Staying True to Your Values

Many businesses may have towering vision and mission statements and value statements, which may include honesty, respect, fairness, transparency, lawfulness, customer satisfaction, and many more values. However, the reality could be starkly different. While pursuing profits in the competitive market, companies may forget their core values and their ethics. Hence, it is important for all businesses to hit pause and take a look at their value systems, their policies, their mission and stay true to their values by avoiding any kind of intentional unethical practice. Companies must also understand their social responsibility and

---

119. "Human Rights in Age of Social Media, Big Data, and AI | National Academies," n.d., https://www.nationalacademies.org/news/2019/09/human-rights-in-age-of-social-media-big-data-and-ai.

do their part towards the well-being of society. You must therefore stay true to your core principles and reevaluate your organization regularly to ensure that you are consistently true to your values and your actions are consistent with your beliefs.

7. Responsiveness

The distinctive feature setting social media apart from other forms of media is its emphasis on engagement and interaction. Users have the ability to pose questions, which can then be answered by fellow users. They can share both positive and negative feedback, as well as address queries and uncertainties. In the event of encountering negative feedback or criticism about you or your products, it would be considered unethical to simply disregard such messages or posts. Ethical conduct entails responding promptly, either by extending a sincere apology or providing a clear explanation. Irrespective of the nature of messages posted on your social media page or in advertisements—be they positive or negative, questions or opinions—it is imperative to maintain responsiveness.

You can post thank you messages for positive reviews or opinions, apology or explanatory messages for negative posts, and an appropriate, satisfactory reply to all messages received on social media.

8. Behaving Responsibly

You carry a huge responsibility towards your stakeholders, owners, customers, suppliers, distributors, and the general public. Hence you must think of the consequences of your posts before posting anything on social media that could hurt any of these stakeholders. You must realize that your posts, messages, and advertisements are visible to a very large audience. Posting anything negative about the stakeholders or posting something that could be detrimental to any of them could have a huge negative impact. The stakeholders may lose trust, discontinue business or take legal action against you, in such a case.

Consider this scenario: if you fail to meet a delivery commitment to a customer who has shared their experience online, and you attribute the issue to distributors, it might provoke a negative reaction from the distributors who could feel offended by such accusations and respond in kind. Similarly, responding discourteously to negative feedback from a customer has the potential to not only upset that customer but also create a detrimental impression among other potential customers. It signals an inability to handle feedback constructively and take responsibility for shortcomings.

9. Avoiding Biases

Everyone has an opinion, especially on social media. However, you have an ethical responsibility to steer away from being biased and opinionated. You must refrain from controversial, hurtful, and demeaning posts. A small mistake could lead to a massive backlash from followers, a huge PR disaster, and a waste of time, money, and effort in doing damage control. Many people have lost their jobs over a single post/tweet. Religious, political, linguistic, cultural, and racial biases should be avoided.

A good example to understand this is that of the world-famous bestselling author J. K. Rowling. She faced massive backlash after she liked a tweet that was considered hateful by the LGBTQ community.[120] The backlash was such that she received a lot of hate mail, lost followers on social media, and people started boycotting her books and movies and demanded an apology from her. She had to give an explanation on her official site[121], the gist of which was that it all began when she accidentally 'liked' a tweet that she intended to screenshot. What followed was a series of tweets explaining her opinion on the issue which made matters worse.

---

120. Abby Gardner, "A Complete Breakdown of the J.K. Rowling Transgender-Comments Controversy," Glamour, October 19, 2023, https://www.glamour.com/story/a-complete-breakdown-of-the-jk-rowling-transgender-comments-controversy.

121. "J.K. Rowling Writes about Her Reasons for Speaking out on Sex and Gender Issues - J.K. Rowling," J.K. Rowling, September 9, 2021, https://www.jkrowling.com/opinions/j-k-rowling-writes-about-her-reasons-for-speaking-out-on-sex-and-gender-issues/.

Exercise

Create a Social Media Code of Ethics

A social media code of ethics is like a rule book and set of guidelines to ensure that a company's social media posts are honest and ethical. If a business is using social media, they should include this as part of their social media marketing plan and share it with anyone who posts on behalf of the company or interacts on its social media channels in any way.

Assume you are the head of a company who needs to prepare the social media code of ethics for your business. Your policy should contain all the 11 social media ethical guidelines explained in Chapter 8 of the book as well as anything else you think is relevant to your values and business. Here are a few examples of social media policies you can use as inspiration:

- The Canadian Bar Association Social Media Policy

- Government of British Columbia Social Media Policy

- Gartner Social Media Policy

- Dell Social Media Policy

Quiz

1. **When a company behaves unethically–**

   a. It creates a positive brand image in the minds of consumers.

   b. Consumers perceive the company and its products and services more positively.

   c. It results in a loss of trust and dissatisfaction among customers.

   d. None of the above.

2. **The following question should be asked related to user privacy–**

   a. Was the consumer's consent taken before accessing his personal data?

   b. Was the consumer made aware of the company's privacy policy?

   c. Does he wish to share his intimate data?

   d. All of the above.

3. **Ethics help improve a company's market position against its immediate competitors.**

   a. True

   b. False

4. Which of the following is correctly related to transparency?

a. Influencers should inform the audience that it is a sponsored review.

b. Influencers must not reveal whether the review is sponsored or not.

c. Influencers must speak only positive things about the products they are reviewing.

d. Influencers should not reveal vital information about the products.

5. _____is an attack that attempts to steal your money, or your identity, by getting you to reveal personal information -- such as credit card numbers, bank information, or passwords -- on websites that pretend to be legitimate.

a. Malware

b. Phishing

c. Drive-by

d. Cryptojacking

6. Unverified claims are ethical as the company does not know whether they are true or not.

a. True

b. False

7. _____helps the company post relevant content.

    a. Being ethical

    b. Defining the target audience

    c. Researching competitor social media campaigns

    d. None of the above

8. **When communication is honest, the audience feels the brand is genuine and trustworthy, thus creating a positive brand image.**

    a. True

    b. False

9. **If some customer comments on the company's social media page with a complaint about late delivery, the company must–**

    a. Make excuses

    b. Question the customer to prove them wrong

    c. Honestly accept its mistake, apologize, and provide a solution.

    d. Delete the comments

10. According to Label Insight, 94% of consumers are likely to be loyal to _____ brands.

    a. transparent

    b. ethical

    c. luxury

    d. economy

Answers	1 − c	2 − d	3 − a	4 − a	5 − b
	6 − b	7 − b	8 − a	9 − c	10 − a

Chapter Summary

◆ The rapid penetration of social media into our lives has raised several questions about ethical social media marketing practices.

◆ Social media marketing is an unprecedented blend of the personal and the professional which provides businesses with extremely intimate consumer data.

◆ Social media marketing ethics can determine how the company is perceived by consumers. It can make or break the brand image of the company or brand in the minds of consumers.

◆ Social media marketers use the data collected by various social media sites to create marketing strategies and target their prospective customers. They need to ensure that they are doing this ethically.

◆ Using ethics in marketing implies using the right conduct, i.e. being fair, unbiased, honest, transparent, and moral in each aspect of marketing like decision making, strategies, behavior, and practice in the organization.

◆ Consumer privacy, lack of transparency, lack of data security, elimination of bias, and sharing misleading or unverified information are some of the major ethical issues in social media marketing.

◆ The best practices for ethical social media marketing include knowing the audience, being honest and transparent, safeguarding customer data, respecting the customers' right to privacy, valuing human rights, staying true to one's values, being responsive, behaving responsibly, avoiding exaggeration, bias and not misleading or misrepresenting.

Bibliography

Mangold, W. Glynn, and David J. Faulds. "Social Media: The New Hybrid Element of the Promotion Mix." Business Horizons 52, no. 4 (July 1, 2009): 357–65. https://doi.org/10.1016/j.bushor.2009.03.002.

Kaplan, Andreas, and Michael Haenlein. "Users of the World, Unite! The Challenges and Opportunities of Social Media." Business Horizons 53, no. 1 (January 1, 2010): 59–68. https://doi.org/10.1016/j.bushor.2009.09.003.

Loc. cit.

Charlesworth, Alan. An Introduction to Social Media Marketing. New York: Routledge, 2014.

Shirey, Trevin. "8 Surprising Social Media Marketing Facts." WebFX, n.d. https://www.webfx.com/blog/social-media/8-surprising-social-media-facts/.

Penguin Team. "68 Social Media Facts & Stats That Will Blow Your Mind." Penguin Strategies, August 3, 2023. https://www.penguinstrategies.com/blog/68-social-media-facts-stats-media-that-will-blow-your-mind.

Ting, Hiram, Winnie Wong Poh Ming, Ernest Cyril De Run, and Sally Lau Yin Choo. "Beliefs about the Use of Instagram: An Exploratory Study." ResearchGate, January 1, 2015. https://www.researchgate.net/publication/272026006_Beliefs_about_the_Use_of_Instagram_An_Exploratory_Study.

Wiechowski, Natalia. "LinkedIn Demystified & Explained: Mind-Blowing Stats, FAQs and Stories." Www.Linkedin.Com, n.d. https://www.linkedin.com/pulse/linkedin-demystified-explained-mind-blowing-stats-faqs-wiechowski.

Newberry, Christina. "42 Facebook Statistics Marketers Need to Know in 2023." Social Media Marketing & Management Dashboard, January 17, 2023. https://blog.hootsuite.com/facebook-statistics/.

Valitova, Svetlana. "Countries with the Most Facebook Users 2023." Ecwid | E-Commerce Shopping Cart, April 28, 2023. https://www.ecwid.com/insights/facebook-countries-with-the-users#:~:text=Most%20active%20Facebook%20users%20in%20India%3A%20329.65%20millions.

Dixon, Stacy. "Number of social media users in the United States from 2019 to 2028." Statista. August 29, 2023. https://www.statista.com/statistics/278409/number-of-social-network-users-in-the-united-states/

Boyd, Danah, and Nicole B. Ellison. "Social Network Sites: Definition, History, and Scholarship." Journal of Computer-Mediated Communication 13, no. 1 (October 1, 2007): 210–30. https://doi.org/10.1111/j.1083-6101.2007.00393.x.

MacMillan, Douglas; McMillan, Robert. "Google Exposed User Data, Feared Repercussions of Disclosing to Public". The Wall Street Journal. October 16, 2018.

Meta. "Introducing Threads: A New Way to Share with Text." Meta, September 7, 2023. https://about.fb.com/news/2023/07/introducing-threads-new-app-text-sharing/.

Rodriguez, Salvador. "Instagram Surpasses 2 Billion Monthly Users While Powering through a Year of Turmoil." CNBC, December 14, 2021. https://www.cnbc.com/2021/12/14/instagram-surpasses-2-billion-monthly-users.html.

Brenner, Claire. "What Is Instagram Marketing? (+7 Instagram Posts That Perform)." Learn.G2.Com, July 26, 2018. https://learn.g2.com/instagram-marketing.

Shepherd, Jack. "23 Essential Twitter Statistics You Need to Know in 2023." The Social Shepherd, May 16, 2023. https://thesocialshepherd.com/blog/twitter-statistics.

Business News Daily. "Everything Your Business Needs to Know about Pinterest," n.d. https://www.businessnewsdaily.com/7552-pinterest-business-guide.htm.l

AlphaStreet. "Pinterest (PINS): A Few Points to Keep in Mind If You Have an Eye on This Stock." AlphaStreet, March 14, 2022. https://news.alphastreet.com/pinterest-pins-a-few-points-to-keep-in-mind-if-you-have-an-eye-on-this-stock/.

About LinkedIn. "About LinkedIn," n.d. https://about.linkedin.com/

Ibid.

Gajić, Ana. "LinkedIn Statistics." 99 firms. n.d. https://99firms.com/blog/linkedin-statistics/#gref.

Macready, Hannah. "47 LinkedIn Statistics You Need To Know In 2023." Social Media Marketing & Management Dashboard, February 22, 2023. https://blog.hootsuite.com/linkedin-statistics-business/.

Bellis, Mary. "The History of Facebook and How It Was Invented." ThoughtCo, February 6, 2020. https://www.thoughtco.com/who-invented-facebook-1991791.

Gajić, Ana ".Instagram Marketing Statistics." 99 Firms. n.d. https://99firms.com/blog/instagram-marketing-statistics/#gref.

Hale, James. "YouTube Viewers Now Watch More Than 1 Billion Hours Of Content Each Day." Tubefilter, May 04, 2021. https://www.tubefilter.com/2021/05/04/youtube-billion-hours-watched-tv-screens-newfronts-2021/ .

Dixon, Stacy. "X (formerly Twitter) accounts with the most followers worldwide as of August 2023." Statista. August 25, 2023. https://www.statista.com/statistics/273172/twitter-accounts-with-the-most-followers-worldwide/.

Osman, Maddy. "Mind-Blowing LinkedIn Statistics and Facts." Kinsta®, September 22, 2023. https://kinsta.com/blog/linkedin-statistics/.

Macready, Hannah. "47 LinkedIn Statistics You Need To Know In 2023." Social Media Marketing & Management Dashboard, February 22, 2023. https://blog.hootsuite.com/linkedin-statistics-business/.

LaFleur, Griffin. "Social Media Marketing (SMM)." WhatIs.Com, October 22, 2021. https://whatis.techtarget.com/definition/social-media-marketing-SMM.

Schaffer, Neal. "55 Compelling Social Media Marketing Statistics You Need To Know For 2023." Social Media & Influencer Marketing Speaker, Consultant & Author, August 11, 2023. https://nealschaffer.com/social-media-marketing-statistics/.

Dencheva, Valentina. "Social media advertising and marketing in the United States - statistics & facts." Statista. August 31, 2023. https://www.statista.com/topics/8791/social-media-marketing-in-the-us/#topicOverview

Panigrahi, Sweta. "Nike's Social Media Strategy: A Deep Dive into Campaigns & Statistics." Keyhole, April 25, 2023. https://keyhole.co/blog/nike-social-media-strategy/.

Ravi, Kavya. "Starbucks' Social Media Strategy - What Brands Can Learn from Starbucks." Unmetric Social Media Analytics Blog, February 12, 2019. https://blog.unmetric.com/starbucks-social-media-strategy.

Sriram, Malathi M. A. "DOVE : Using Social Media for Social Viral Campaign - A Case Study." Shri Dharmasthala Manjunatheshwara Research Centre for Management Studies (SDM RCMS), SDMIMD, Mysore, Accessed June 06, 2023 : https://www.sdmimd.ac.in/SDMRCMS/cases/CIM2013/3.pdf.

IFP. "How Oreo's Adaptable Strategy Helps Them Dominate Social Media." August 30, 2021. https://www.insightsforprofessionals.com/marketing/social-media/how-oreo-dominates-social-media.

Responsival. "Lessons from Sephora — Marketing Across Multiple Channels." November, 2021. https://www.responsival.com/post/lessons-from-sephora-marketing-across-multiple-channels.

Stroud, Samuel. "GoPro Social Media: How Did It Become so Successful?" Giraffe Social - Social Media Agency, October 23, 2023. https://www.giraffesocialmedia.co.uk/gopro-social-media-how-did-it-become-so-successful/.

IvyPanda. "Airbnb: Social Media Strategy - 1223 Words | Essay Example," June 13, 2021. https://ivypanda.com/essays/airbnb-social-media-strategy/.

Panigrahi, Sweta. "Netflix's Winning Social Media Strategy: A Deep Dive." Keyhole, December 13, 2023. https://keyhole.co/blog/netflixs-winning-social-media-strategy-a-deep-dive/#:~:text=Netflix's%20social%20media%20strategy%20involves,from%20their%20top%2Dperforming%20shows.

Tumminello, Lauren. "Social Media ROI Case Study - AHBA | Firefly Marketing." Firefly Marketing (blog), n.d. https://marketwithfirefly.com/does-social-media-make-sense-for-my-roi/.

Kraus, Elizabeth, and Audrey Rawnie Rico. "Everything You Need to Know about TV Advertising Costs." Fit Small Business (blog), March 14, 2023. https://fitsmallbusiness.com/tv-advertising/.

Kotler P., Keller K.L., Koshy A., Jha M., 2009 Marketing Management – A South Asian Perspective, 14 E., Pearson, Delhi.

Ibid

Clow Kenneth E., Baack Donald, 2004, Integrated Advertising, Promotion & Marketing Communications, New Delhi, Prentice Hall of India.

Shah K., D'Souza A., 2009, Advertising and Promotion- An IMC Perspective, Tata McGraw Hill, New Delhi.

Gartner. "Definition of Media Mix - Gartner Marketing Glossary," n.d. https://www.gartner.com/en/marketing/glossary/media-mix#:~:text=A%20media%20mix%20is%20the,TV%20ads%20and%20direct%20email.

Chunawalla S. A., Sethia K. C. (2008) Foundations of Advertising, Mumbai, Himalaya Publishing House.

Chattopadhyay, Tanmay, Rudrendu Narayan Dutta, and Shradha Sivani. "Media Mix Elements Affecting Brand Equity: A Study of the Indian Passenger Car Market." IIMB Management Review 22, no. 4 (December 1, 2010): 173–85. https://doi.org/10.1016/j.iimb.2010.09.001.

Staff, Morning Consult. "The Influencer Report." Morning Consult Pro, October, 2019. https://pro.morningconsult.com/analyst-reports/influencer-report.

Meta. "Sharing Photos and Videos." Help Centre, Meta. https://help.instagram.com/488619974671134/?helpref=hc_fnav.

O'Brien, Clodagh. "How to Develop a Social Media Strategy That Drives Brand Awareness & ROI." Digital Marketing Institute, April 11, 2022. https://digitalmarketinginstitute.com/blog/social-media-strategy.

Opresnik, Marc Oliver. "Effective Social Media Marketing Planning – How to Develop a Digital Marketing Plan." In: Meiselwitz, G. (eds) Social Computing and Social Media. User Experience and Behavior. SCSM. Lecture Notes in Computer Science (), Vol. 10913. Springer, Cham. (May 2018): 333-341. https://doi.org/10.1007/978-3-319-91521-0_24.

Evolve. "How Much Should I Spend On Social Media Marketing?" Evolve Media, n.d. https://evolvemedia.com/how-much-should-i-spend-on-social-media-marketing/.

Dencheva, Valentina. "Share of marketing budgets devoted to social media marketing according to CMOs in the United States from 2015 to 2024." Statista. July 04, 2023. https://www.statista.com/statistics/1223663/social-media-marketing-budget-share-usa/.

Holly Ringerud. "Social Media Mission Statements: What Are They & How Do They Help Your Social Strategy?" Tallwave. November 12, 2020. https://tallwave.com/blog/social-media-mission-statements-what-are-they-how-do-they-help-your-social-strategy/#:~:text=Your%20social%20mission%20statement%20should,Comment%3F.

Tien, Shannon. "13 Easy Ways To Tackle Social Media Optimization." Social Media Marketing & Management Dashboard, November 23, 2023. https://blog.hootsuite.com/social-media-optimization/.

Hanaysha, Jalal Rajeh. "Impact of Social Media Marketing Features on Consumer's Purchase Decision in the Fast-Food Industry: Brand Trust as a Mediator." International Journal of Information Management Data Insights 2, no. 2 (November 1, 2022): 100102. https://doi.org/10.1016/j.jjimei.2022.100102.

Ahmad, Nur Syakirah, Rosidah Musa, and Mior Harris Mior Harun. "The Impact of Social Media Content Marketing (SMCM) towards Brand Health." Procedia. Economics and Finance 37 (January 1, 2016): 331–36. https://doi.org/10.1016/s2212-5671(16)30133-2.

Atkinson, Olivia. "What Is Blogging And Why Is It Important For Building Material Businesses?" Insynth (blog), March 20, 2019. https://www.insynth.co.uk/blog/what-is-a-blogging-and-why-is-it-important-for-building-material-businesses.

Paruch, Zach. "12 Types of Content Marketing to Leverage for Success in 2023." Semrush Blog, May 3, 2023. https://www.semrush.com/blog/types-of-content-marketing/.

Sarda, Pranit. "Gaurav Chaudhary: Your 'Technical Guruji'" Forbes India, February 12, 2020. https://www.forbesindia.com/article/30-under-30-2020/gaurav-chaudhary-your-039technical-guruji039/57639/1.

Rouse, Margaret. "Podcast." Techopedia. October 16, 2013. https://www.techopedia.com/definition/5546/podcast

Corporate Communications, Inc. "The Benefits of Live Video on Social Media," n.d. https://www.corporatecomm.com/blog/the-benefits-of-live-video-on-social-media.

Gajić, Ana. "28 Facebook Live Stats to Know in 2023". 99Firms, n.d. https://99firms.com/blog/facebook-live-stats/#gref

Dopson, Elise. "The Shift in Your Content Marketing Mix: 25 Marketers On What's Changed in 2 Years | Databox Blog." Databox, October 9, 2023. https://databox.com/perfect-content-marketing-mix#:~:text=Mix%20in%202021-,What%20is%20a%20Content%20Mix%3F,and%20retain%20your%20ideal%20customers.

BigCommerce. "Facebook Marketing for Ecommerce: What It Means and Best Practices," n.d. https://www.bigcommerce.com/ecommerce-answers/what-is-facebook-marketing/ .

Shepherd, Jack. "33 Essential Facebook Statistics You Need to Know in 2023". Social Shepherd. June 26, 2023. https://thesocialshepherd.com/blog/facebook-statistics#:~:text=An%20average%20of%20100%20million,video%20views%20are%20gained%20daily.

Facebook Business. "Introducing Facebook Stories Ads." Meta. September 26, 2018. https://en-gb.facebook.com/business/news/introducing-facebook-stories-ads

Golob, Leah. "How to Use Facebook Stories for Business: The Complete Guide." Social Media Marketing & Management Dashboard, March 16, 2021. https://blog.hootsuite.com/facebook-stories/

Meta. "Create lightweight, affordable video ads from images that you already have," n.d. 2023. https://en-gb.facebook.com/business/ads/slideshow-ad-format#

Meta. "Investing $1 Billion in Creators." July 14, 2021. https://about.fb.com/news/2021/07/investing-1-billion-dollars-in-creators/

Berry, Sarah. "How Much Does Facebook Advertising Cost in 2023?" WebFX, n.d. https://www.webfx.com/social-media/pricing/how-much-does-facebook-advertising-cost/.

Dixon, Stacy Jo. "Distribution of Instagram users worldwide as of January 2023, by age group." Statista. August 25, 2023. https://www.statista.com/statistics/325587/instagram-global-age-group/

Decker, Allie. "Instagram Marketing." Hubspot, n.d. https://www.hubspot.com/instagram-marketing

Instagram Business Team. "Get the latest from Instagram." Meta. September 10, 2021. https://business.instagram.com/blog/instagram-business-insights-creativity?locale=en_GB

Meta. "Record a Reel on Instagram," n.d. https://help.instagram.com/2720958398006062

Meta. "New video Posts on Instagram will be shared as Reels." July 26, 2022. https://business.instagram.com/blog/instagram-video-now-instagram-reels?locale=en_GB

Meta. "Flex With An Impactful Video Strategy," n.d. https://business.instagram.com/ad-solutions/video-strategy

Meta. "Photo ads-Inspire people with an easy-to-make photo ad," n.d. https://www.facebook.com/business/ads/photo-ad-format

Geyser, Werner. "How Much Does It Cost to Advertise on Instagram?" Influencer Marketing Hub, June 8, 2022. https://influencermarketinghub.com/instagram-ads-cost/.

Patel, Neil. "How Much Do Instagram Ads Cost in 2023?" Neil Patel, n.d. https://neilpatel.com/blog/instagram-ads-prices/.

Andony, Brock. "Organic Twitter Marketing: The Fundamental Guide - Vendasta Blog." Vendasta Blog, November 2, 2020. https://www.vendasta.com/blog/organic-twitter-marketing/.

X Business. "What are Promoted Ads?" n.d. https://business.twitter.com/en/help/overview/what-are-promoted-ads.html

X Business. "X Ad Formats," n.d. https://business.twitter.com/en/advertising/formats.html#amplify-twitter.

X Business. "Trend Takeover and Trend Takeover+ Your ad placed alongside what's trending" n.d. https://business.twitter.com/en/advertising/takeover/trend-takeovers.html

Heath, Alex, and Mia Sato. "Hundreds of Twitter Employees Resign after Elon Musk's 'Hardcore' Ultimatum." The Verge, November 18, 2022. https://www.theverge.com/2022/11/17/23465274/hundreds-of-twitter-employees-resign-from-elon-musk-hardcore-deadline.

Sweney, Mark. "Twitter 'to Lose 32m Users in Two Years after Elon Musk Takeover.'" The Guardian, December 13, 2022. https://www.theguardian.com/technology/2022/dec/13/twitter-lose-users-elon-musk-takeover-hate-speech.

Farley, Nicole. "How Brands and Agencies Are Reacting to Elon Musk's Radical Changes at Twitter." Search Engine Land, November 2, 2022. https://searchengineland.com/twitter-advertising-elon-musk-brands-agencies-389311.

Levin, Matt. "To Tweet or Not to Tweet? How Brands Are Wrestling with Elon Musk's Twitter." Marketplace, December 16, 2022. https://www.marketplace.org/2022/12/16/how-brands-are-wrestling-with-elon-musks-twitter/.

Kann, Sharon and Karusone, Angelo. " In less than a month, Elon Musk has driven away half of Twitter's top 100 advertisers." Media Matters. November 22, 2022. https://www.mediamatters.org/elon-musk/less-month-elon-musk-has-driven-away-half-twitters-top-100-advertisers

Pintado, Amanda Perez. "Half of Twitter's top advertisers have left the platform since Elon Musk's takeover, report says." USA Today. November 28, 2022. https://www.usatoday.com/story/tech/2022/11/28/twitter-loses-advertisers-after-elon-musk/10790189002/

Harwell, Drew. "A Fake Tweet Sparked Panic at Eli Lilly and May Have Cost Twitter Millions." The Washington Post. November 14, 2022. https://www.washingtonpost.com/technology/2022/11/14/twitter-fake-eli-lilly/

Dang, Sheila. "Exclusive: Twitter to Introduce New Controls for Ad Placements." Reuters, December 10, 2022. https://www.reuters.com/technology/twitter-introduce-new-controls-ad-placements-email-2022-12-09/.

Growleady. "'4 out of 5 Users on LinkedIn Drive Business Decisions' - What Does This Mean for Marketers and How Can You Make the Most out of It in Your Outreach?," n.d. https://www.linkedin.com/pulse/4-out-5-users-linkedin-drive-business-decisions-what-does-/.

LinkedIn Marketing Solutions. "LinkedIn Pages." LinkedIn, n.d. https://business.linkedin.com/marketing-solutions/cx/22/02/linkedin-pages-sr-d

LinkedIn. "Opt out of Sponsored Messaging." May 2023. https://www.linkedin.com/help/linkedin/answer/62649/opt-out-of-sponsored-messaging#:~:text=LinkedIn%20Sponsored%20Messaging%20is%3A,personal%20or%20professional%20email%20inbox.

Hayden, John. "LinkedIn Dynamic Ads Are Now Available in Campaign Manager." Digital Marketing Community. Accessed: October 10, 2023. https://www.digitalmarketingcommunity.com/news/linkedin-dynamic-ads-are-now-available-in-campaign-manager/

LinkedIn. "Text Ads." n.d. https://business.linkedin.com/marketing-solutions/ppc-advertising

Team, WebFX. "How Much Does LinkedIn Advertising Cost in 2023?" WebFX, n.d, 2023. https://www.webfx.com/social-media/pricing/how-much-does-linkedin-advertising-cost/.

Mohsin, Maryam. "10 YouTube Statistics That You Need to Know in 2023." Oberlo (blog), June 20, 2023. https://www.oberlo.com/blog/youtube-statistics.

Loc. cit.

Pinterest. "Feed Optimization Playbook." n.d. https://assets.ctfassets.net/h67z7i6sbjau/3IY6IiM0GhGeEYVIz3Tjnc/ 58cb4970482cfe9cc7f48dfb41e88123/Feed_optimization_guide_2021.pdf

Pinterest. "Pinterest For Business: How to Market Your Brand \ | Pinterest Business," n.d. https://business.pinterest.com/en-in/.

Pinterest. "Advertising on Pinterest | Pinterest Business," n.d. https://business.pinterest.com/en-in/advertise/.

Pinterest Help. "Video Ads," n.d. https://help.pinterest.com/en/business/article/promoted-video-with-autoplay

WebFX. "How Much Does Pinterest Advertising Cost in 2023?" WebFX, n.d, 2023. https://www.webfx.com/social-media/pricing/how-much-does-pinterest-advertising-cost/.

108. Sedhai, Surendra, and Sun, Aixin. "Hashtag recommendation for hyperlinked tweets."SIGIR '14: Proceedings of the International ACM SIGIR Conference on Research and Development in Information Retrieval. (July, 2014):831-834. https://www.researchgate.net/publication/266658631_Hashtag_recommendation_for_hyperlinked_tweets

BrightEdge. "Social Media Metrics," n.d. https://www.brightedge.com/glossary/social-media-metrics.

Tegze, Jan. "Why Your LinkedIn Posts Matter More than You Think." September 14, 2022. https://jantegze.com/blog/why-your-linkedin-posts-matter-more-than-you-think/.

Newberry, Christina. "16 Key Social Media Metrics to Track in 2023 [BENCHMARKS]" June 23, 2022. https://blog.hootsuite.com/social-media-metrics/

Lavinsky, Dave. "Influencer Marketing Metrics You Should Be Tracking - Supermetrics," November 17, 2021. https://supermetrics.com/blog/influencer-marketing-metrics.

Grand View Research. "Influencer Marketing Platform Market Size, Share & Trends Analysis Report By Application, By Organization Size, By End-Use, By Region, And Segment Forecasts, 2022 - 2030," n.d. https://www.grandviewresearch.com/industry-analysis/influencer-marketing-platform-market.

Wong, Laura. "How to Prove (and Improve!) Your Social Media ROI." Hootsuite. September 21, 2023. https://blog.hootsuite.com/measure-social-media-roi-business/

SocialBee. "Traffic Meaning | Social Media Marketing Glossary," n.d. https://socialbee.io/glossary/traffic/.

Sprout Social. "What Is Net Promoter Score (NPS)? | Sprout Social," n.d. https://sproutsocial.com/glossary/net-promoter-score/.

Influencer Marketing Hub. "What Is Net Promoter Score (NPS)?," n.d. https://influencermarketinghub.com/glossary/net-promoter-score-nps/.

Dincer, Caner, and Banu Dinçer. "An Overview and Analysis of Marketing Ethics." International Journal of Academic Research in Business & Social Sciences 4, no. 11 (November 25, 2014): 151-158. http://dx.doi.org/10.6007/IJARBSS/v4-i11/1290

Dhole, V.S. "Ethics in Marketing." Vidyabharati International Interdisciplinary Research Journal 9(2). (December 2019): 155-157. https://www.researchgate.net/profile/Vikas-Dole-3/publication/354651377_ETHICS_IN_MARKETING/links/6144435ad5f4292c01fe8ae3/ETHICS-IN-MARKETING.pdf

Microsoft. "Protect yourself from phishing." n.d. https://support.microsoft.com/en-us/windows/protect-yourself-from-phishing-0c7ea947-ba98-3bd9-7184-430e1f860a44

Research Briefs. "#Fail: 29 Of The Biggest Corporate Brand Social Media Flubs." March 17, 2017. https://www.cbinsights.com/research/corporate-social-media-fails/

Barber, Daniel. "Why Brands That Opt For Transparency Are Winning." Forbes. Dec 29, 2020. https://www.forbes.com/sites/forbestechcouncil/2021/12/29/why-brands-that-opt-for-transparency-are-winning/?sh=33dc26db451e

Chatterjee, Aneeka. "Instagram: Meta hit with €405 million over children's data breach." Businessline. September 06, 2022. https://www.thehindubusinessline.com/info-tech/social-media/instagram-meta-hit-with-405-million-over-childrens-data-breach/article65856700.ece

Korff, Douwe, Brown, Ian. "Social Media and Human Rights." Commissioner for Human Rights, Strasbourg. February, 2012. https://rm.coe.int/16806da579

Galvin, Molly "Human Rights in Age of Social Media, Big Data, and AI." National Academies. September 23, 2019. https://www.nationalacademies.org/news/2019/09/human-rights-in-age-of-social-media-big-data-and-ai

Gardner, Abby. "A Complete Breakdown of the J.K. Rowling Transgender-Comments Controversy." Glamour, October 19, 2023. https://www.glamour.com/story/a-complete-breakdown-of-the-jk-rowling-transgender-comments-controversy.

Rowling, J.K. "J.K. Rowling Writes about Her Reasons for Speaking Out on Sex and Gender Issues." J.K Rowling. June 10, 2020. www.jkrowling.com/opinions/j-k-rowling-writes-about-her-reasons-for-speaking-out-on-sex-and-gender-issues/

www.ingramcontent.com/pod-product-compliance
Lightning Source LLC
Chambersburg PA
CBHW050338270326
41926CB00016B/3508